First World War
and Army of Occupation
War Diary
France, Belgium and Germany

42 DIVISION
126 Infantry Brigade,
Brigade Machine Gun Company
1 March 1917 - 28 February 1918

WO95/2658/3

The Naval & Military Press Ltd
www.nmarchive.com
Published in association with The National Archives

Published by

The Naval & Military Press Ltd

Unit 10 Ridgewood Industrial Park,

Uckfield, East Sussex,

TN22 5QE England

Tel: +44 (0) 1825 749494

www.naval-military-press.com

www.nmarchive.com

This diary has been reprinted in facsimile from the original. Any imperfections are inevitably reproduced and the quality may fall short of modern type and cartographic standards.

© Crown Copyright
Images reproduced by permission of The National Archives, London, England, 2015.

Contents

Document type	Place/Title	Date From	Date To
Heading	WO95/2658 126 Inf Bgde Bgde MGC Mar 17-Feb. 18		
Heading	42nd Division 126th Infy Bde 126th Machine Gun Coy Mar 1917-Feb 1918		
Heading	No. 126 Machine Gun Coy. Period From 1st March 1917 To 31st March 1917 Vol XII		
War Diary	At Sea	01/03/1917	05/03/1917
War Diary	Marseilles	06/03/1917	06/03/1917
War Diary	On Board Train	07/03/1917	07/03/1917
War Diary	Pont Remy	08/03/1917	08/03/1917
War Diary	St. Maxent	09/03/1917	30/03/1917
War Diary	Liercourt	31/03/1917	31/03/1917
Heading	No 126 Machine Gun Company. From 1st April 1917 To 30th April 1917. Vol XIII		
War Diary	Liercourt.	01/04/1917	07/04/1917
War Diary	Morcourt	08/04/1917	11/04/1917
War Diary	Frise	12/04/1917	17/04/1917
War Diary	Peronne	18/04/1917	18/04/1917
War Diary	Longavesnes	19/04/1917	20/04/1917
War Diary	Pieziere.	21/04/1917	30/04/1917
Heading	No 126 Machine Gun Coy. From 1st May 1917 To 31st May 1917. Vol XIV		
War Diary	Longavesnes.	01/05/1917	13/05/1917
War Diary	St Emilie	14/05/1917	17/05/1917
War Diary	Longavesnes	18/05/1917	19/05/1917
War Diary	Equancourt	20/05/1917	20/05/1917
War Diary	Neuville	21/05/1917	21/05/1917
War Diary	Havrincourt Wood Q 13.d.48	22/05/1917	31/05/1917
War Diary	No. 126th Machine Gun Coy. Vol 5, Period 1st June 1917 To 30th June 1917.		
War Diary	Havrincourt Wood (Q 13a 4.8)	01/06/1917	05/06/1917
War Diary	Havrincourt Wood.	06/06/1917	06/06/1917
War Diary	Ytres.	07/06/1917	21/06/1917
War Diary	Ytres-Havrincourt Wood	22/06/1917	22/06/1917
War Diary	Havrincourt Wood.	23/06/1917	30/06/1917
Heading	No 126 Machine Gun Coy Vol 6 Period 1 July 1917 To 31st July 1917 Vol 6		
War Diary	Havrincourt Wood	01/07/1917	07/07/1917
War Diary	Ytres.	08/07/1917	08/07/1917
War Diary	Ytres Bihucourt	09/07/1917	09/07/1917
War Diary	Bihucourt	10/07/1917	11/07/1917
War Diary	Courcelles	12/07/1917	31/07/1917
Miscellaneous	126. Machine Gun Company.		
Miscellaneous	Appendix II		
Operation(al) Order(s)	Operation Order 14 by Major E.R.M. Kirkpatrick Comdg 126th M.G.M.	10/07/1917	10/07/1917
Miscellaneous	Appendix III		
Miscellaneous			
Miscellaneous	Appendix I.		
Miscellaneous	Made to water a hall will be made at Bapaume to water in fuel		

Type	Description	Start	End
Miscellaneous	Operation Order No 13 No 5	08/07/1917	08/07/1917
Miscellaneous	Appendix. N		
Miscellaneous	126. Machine Gun Company Programme of training for week ending Training.		
Miscellaneous	Appendix V		
Miscellaneous	126th Machine Gun Company Brigade Of Training For Week Ending 27 August 1917		
Heading	No. 126. M.G. Coy Vol 7 Period 1st August 1917 To 31st August 1917 Vol XVII		
War Diary	Courcelles.	01/08/1917	21/08/1917
War Diary	Bertrancourt	22/08/1917	22/08/1917
War Diary	Watou. W. Flanders	23/08/1917	30/08/1917
War Diary	Ypres	31/08/1917	31/08/1917
Heading	No 126 Machine Gun Company Vol 8 Period 1st September 1917 To 30th September 1917. Vol XVII		
War Diary	Ypres	01/09/1917	16/09/1917
War Diary	Brandhoek	16/09/1917	19/09/1917
War Diary	Winnizeele	20/09/1917	21/09/1917
War Diary	Wormhoudt.	22/09/1917	22/09/1917
War Diary	Zuydcoote	23/09/1917	23/09/1917
War Diary	La Panne	24/09/1917	24/09/1917
War Diary	Surrey Camp	25/09/1917	30/09/1917
Operation(al) Order(s)	126 Machine Gun Company Order No. 16 By Major E.R.M. Kirkpatrick.	01/09/1917	01/09/1917
Miscellaneous	Appendix No 2		
Operation(al) Order(s)	Operation Order By Major E.R.M. Kirkpatrick. Commanding 126 Machine Gun Company.	07/09/1917	07/09/1917
Miscellaneous	Appendix No. III.		
Miscellaneous	Operation Order By Major E.R.M. Kirkpatrick. Commanding 126 Machine Gun Company.	11/09/1917	11/09/1917
Operation(al) Order(s)	Operation Order No 11 By Major E.R.M. Kirkpatrick. Commanding 126 Machine Gun Company.	12/09/1917	12/09/1917
Miscellaneous	Appendix No V		
Miscellaneous	Appendix No IV		
Miscellaneous	Orders For Move By Major E.R.M. Kirkpatrick Commanding 126 Machine Gun Company	20/09/1917	20/09/1917
Miscellaneous	Orders For Move By Major E.R.M. Kirkpatrick Commanding 126 Machine Gun Company	18/09/1917	18/09/1917
Miscellaneous	Appendix No VI.		
Miscellaneous	Appendix No VII		
Miscellaneous	Orders For Move By Major E.R.M. Kirkpatrick. Commanding 126 Machine Gun Company.	23/09/1917	23/09/1917
Heading	No 126 Machine Gun Company Vol 9 Period 1 October 1917 To 31st October 1917. Vol XIX		
War Diary	Surrey Camp. R. 32.c.5.6.	01/10/1917	06/10/1917
War Diary	Coxyde	07/10/1917	07/10/1917
War Diary	Nieuport	08/10/1917	31/10/1917
Operation(al) Order(s)	126 Machine Gun Company Order No. 25	01/10/1917	01/10/1917
Miscellaneous	Appendix II.		
Operation(al) Order(s)	126 Machine Gun Company Order No. 26	03/10/1917	03/10/1917
Miscellaneous	Appendix III		
Operation(al) Order(s)	126 Machine Gun Company Order No. 27 App III	05/10/1917	05/10/1917
Miscellaneous	Appendix IV		
Operation(al) Order(s)	126 Machine Gun Company Order No. 28 App IV	06/10/1917	06/10/1917
Miscellaneous	Appendix V		
Operation(al) Order(s)	Remnant Company Order No. 32 App V	13/10/1917	13/10/1917

Type	Description	Start	End
Miscellaneous	Appendix. VI		
Operation(al) Order(s)	Remnant Company Order No.35. App VI	15/10/1917	15/10/1917
Miscellaneous	Appendix VII		
Operation(al) Order(s)	Remnant Company Order No. 37	16/10/1917	16/10/1917
Miscellaneous	Appendix VIII		
Operation(al) Order(s)	Remnant Company Order No. 39.	16/10/1917	16/10/1917
Miscellaneous	Appendix IX		
Operation(al) Order(s)	Remnant Operation Order No. 42	19/10/1917	19/10/1917
Miscellaneous	Appendix X		
Operation(al) Order(s)	Remnant Order No. 46.	17/10/1917	17/10/1917
Operation(al) Order(s)	Remnant Operation Order No. 52.	23/10/1917	23/10/1917
Miscellaneous	Appendix XII.		
Operation(al) Order(s)	Remnant Order No.55	27/10/1917	27/10/1917
Miscellaneous	Appendix XIII		
Operation(al) Order(s)	Remnant Order No.51	31/10/1917	31/10/1917
Heading	No 126 Machine Gun Company Vol 10 Period 1st Nov 1917 To 30th Nov 1917 Vol XX		
War Diary	Nieuport	01/11/1917	20/11/1917
War Diary	Hardifort	21/11/1917	21/11/1917
War Diary	Staple.	22/11/1917	22/11/1917
War Diary	Warne	23/11/1917	27/11/1917
War Diary	Molinghem	28/11/1917	28/11/1917
War Diary	Bethune.	29/11/1917	30/11/1917
Operation(al) Order(s)	Remnant Order No. 64	02/11/1917	02/11/1917
Operation(al) Order(s)	Remnant Order No. 65.	07/11/1917	07/11/1917
Miscellaneous	Appendix II		
Operation(al) Order(s)	126 Machine Gun Company Order No. 66.	17/11/1917	17/11/1917
Operation(al) Order(s)	126 Machine Gun Company Order No. 70.	18/11/1917	18/11/1917
Heading	No 126 Machine Gun Company Vol 11 Period 1st Dec 1917 To 31st Dec 1917 Vol XXI		
War Diary	Bethune	01/12/1917	10/12/1917
War Diary	La Bassee	11/12/1917	31/12/1917
Miscellaneous	Appendix I		
Operation(al) Order(s)	126 Machine Gun Company Order No. 75	09/12/1917	09/12/1917
Heading	No 126 M. Gun. Coy Vol 12, Period 1st Jan 1918 To 31st Jan 1918 Vol XXII		
War Diary	La Bassee	01/01/1918	04/01/1918
War Diary	Essars	05/01/1918	18/01/1918
War Diary	Le Plantin	19/01/1918	31/01/1918
Miscellaneous	Appendix I		
Operation(al) Order(s)	126 Machine Gun Company Order No. 76	02/01/1918	02/01/1918
Miscellaneous	Appendix II		
Operation(al) Order(s)	126 Machine Gun Company Order No. 77	13/01/1918	13/01/1918
Heading	No. 126 Machine Gun Coy. Period 1st February 1918 To 28th February 1918 Vol XXIII		
War Diary	Le Plantin	01/02/1918	13/02/1918
War Diary	Le Plantin In La Beuvriere	14/02/1918	14/02/1918
War Diary	Labeuvriere	15/02/1918	28/02/1918

WO95/2658 (3)

126 INF BDE
BDE MGC
Mar'17 - Feb'18

42ND DIVISION
126TH INFY BDE

126TH MACHINE GUN COY

MAR 1917 - FEB 1918

42ND DIVISION
126TH INFY BDE

Army Form C. 2118.

Confidential

Vol 2

WAR DIARY
or
INTELLIGENCE SUMMARY
(Erase heading not required.)

No. 126 Machine Gun Coy.

Vol. XII

Period From 1st March 1917
To 31st March 1917

Ref. Maps:-
ABBEVILLE 1/4.
1/100,000.

Place	Date	Hour	Summary of Events and Information	Remarks and references to Appendices

Army Form C. 2118.

WAR DIARY
or
INTELLIGENCE SUMMARY
(Erase heading not required.)

No. 126 Machine Gun Coy.

Place	Date	Hour	Summary of Events and Information	Remarks and references to Appendices
AT SEA	1917 1st & 2nd Mch		Nothing to report	
AT SEA	3rd Mch		Arrived MALTA during night. 2/3 Mch. Held Kit inspection. Sailed 1000.	
AT SEA	4th & 5th Mch		Nothing to report.	
MARSEILLES	6th Mch		0830 Arrived MARSEILLE. disembarked, entrained and left for PONT REMY 1500	
ON BOARD TRAIN	7th Mch		Nothing to report	
PONT REMY	8th Mch	2230	Arrived PONT REMY Station + detrained	
ST. MAXENT	9th Mch		Left PONT REMY 0630 by march route and arrived ST MAXENT 0450. Men all billeted in one farm. 2nd Lt. HAMPSON and 4 O.R. with riding horses rejoined.	
ST. MAXENT	10th Mch		Drew felled blanket from Advanced Stores Depot ABBEVILLE :- 12 G.S. limbers, 1 m/cart, 1 mess cart and 47 horses.	
ST. MAXENT	11th Mch		M. Fleurelle (interpreter) reported for attachment.	
ST. MAXENT	12th Mch		Drew from Ordnance, PONT REMY, 16 Vickers guns with equipment total labels, and cardigans for company	
ST. MAXENT	13th Mch		Drew from Delisieux, PONT REMY, gun equipment for coy. also 4 Bicycles, & 16 haversacks	
ST. MAXENT	14th Mch		Coy. in marching order with transport & inspected by Brigadier at HUPPY. Secured a reception room in village for men	
ST. MAXENT	15th Mch		Nothing to report. Man admitted sick to hospital for half amount enrolled to-day. 1 D. + 8 O.R.	
ST. MAXENT	16th Mch		2 O.R. granted furlough to U.K. Left for BOULOGNE. Drew out one G.S. limber & two horses	
ST. MAXENT	17th Mch		LT. BRIGHS with 3 O.R. who left EGYPT as advance party rejoined coy from a period of instruction with No. 2 M.G. Coy on joining here. LT. BLEARLEY with 2 O.R. left for a course of instruction with the same coy.	

Army Form C. 2118.

WAR DIARY
or
INTELLIGENCE SUMMARY
(Erase heading not required.)

Instructions regarding War Diaries and Intelligence Summaries are contained in F. S. Regs., Part II. and the Staff Manual respectively. Title Pages will be prepared in manuscript.

Place	Date	Hour	Summary of Events and Information	Remarks and references to Appendices
	1917		No. 126 Machine Gun Coy.	
ST MAXENT	18th Mch		Sunday - resting.	
ST MAXENT	19th Mch		Capt. Gillies and Lt. Kelly attended conference of officers at Bde H.Q. with Major General. Capt. Beer assumed L/C Camiers in M.G. course of instruction.	
ST MAXENT	20th Mch 21st Mch		Training.	
ST MAXENT	22nd Mch		Inspection of transport by Capt. Aris, O.C. 430th Coy. A.S.C. Coln.	
ST MAXENT	23rd Mch		Lt. Beazley and 2 O.R. returned from period of instruction in Tanks.	
ST MAXENT	24th Mch		Training.	
ST MAXENT	25th Mch		Capt. Gillies proceeded to Grantham for course of instruction, leaving Pont Remy Station 0625. F. Arthur Gillies Capt. O.C. 126 M.G. Coy.	
CT MAXENT	26th Mch		Enemy Artillery Support. Field Firing Doulancotte.	
"	27th Mch		Field Firing Doulancotte. Major E.R.M. Kirkpatrick assumed command of the Coy.	
"	28th Mch		Training.	
"	29th Mch		Training. Lecture by Divisional Gas Officer - a Lethargy Liveness of small box respirators.	
"	30th Mch		Company moved into billets at Liercourt - (Somme)	
LIERCOURT	31st Mch		Training. E.R.M. Kirkpatrick Major O.C. 126 M.G. Coy.	

Army Form C. 2118.

WAR DIARY
INTELLIGENCE SUMMARY
(Erase heading not required.)

Vol 3

No. 126. MACHINE GUN COMPANY.

Vol XIII

Period.

FROM 1st April 1917.
TO 30th April 1917.

Ref. Maps.
Abbeville 14.   1/100,000
Amiens 17.   1/100,000
62 c. NE   1/20,000
57 c. SE   1/20,000

Place	Date	Hour	Summary of Events and Information	Remarks and references to Appendices

Army Form C. 2118.

WAR DIARY
INTELLIGENCE SUMMARY
(Erase heading not required.)

Place	Date 1917	Hour	Summary of Events and Information	Remarks and references to Appendices
LIERCOURT	Oct. 1st		Sunday. nothing to report.	S/Mill
LIERCOURT	Oct. 2nd		Range firing PONT REMY.	S/Mill
"	Oct. 3rd		Training	S/Mill
"	Oct. 4th		Range firing PONT REMY.	S/Mill
"	Oct. 5th		Nothing to report. Draft of 30 men arrived from M.G.C. Base Depot Camiers	S/Mill
"	Oct. 6th		Transport proceeded by road to Neufbillets at MORCOURT	S/Mill
"	Oct. 7th		Company moved to MORCOURT by rail	S/Mill
MORCOURT	Oct. 8th		Nothing to report	S/Mill
MORCOURT	Oct. 9th		Training	S/Mill
"	Oct. 10th		Training. 59 men attached to Company for training arrived from Base from the Brigade	S/Mill
"	Oct. 11th		Company moved by march route to FRISE	S/Mill
FRISE	Oct. 12th		Training.	S/Mill
"	Oct. 13th		Conference of C.O's. Rifle HQrs. Draft of 8 men reported from M.G.C. Base depot Camiers	S/Mill

Army Form C. 2118.

WAR DIARY
or
INTELLIGENCE SUMMARY

(Erase heading not required.)

Instructions regarding War Diaries and Intelligence
Summaries are contained in F. S. Regs., Part II.
and the Staff Manual respectively. Title Pages
will be prepared in manuscript.

Place	Date	Hour	Summary of Events and Information	Remarks and references to Appendices
FRISE	Apr 14th		Training	
"	Apr 15th		Training	
"	Apr 16th		Nothing to report. Training	
"	" 17th		Company moved by march route to PERONNE	
PERONNE	" 18th		Company moved by march route to LONGAVESNES	
LONGAVESNES	Apr 19th		Training	
"	" 20th		Training	
PEIZIERE	" 21st		Company moved to PEIZIERE. To relieve 143rd Machine Gun Coy on the line. One section in Right Sector and one section in Left Sector. Two sections in defence of Brown line. Right Boundary of 126th Bde. F.13 central – MAY COPSE (exclusive) 200 yards N of TOMBOIS FARM and through F.6.c.1.0. Left Boundary :- from the railway at X.19.c.2.0. to (R) through the "R" of RAVINE at X.16.c.6.7.	
"	Apr 22nd		No 1 gun, No 1 Section buried by direct hit (F.5.a.18.) out of action 12 hours. No Casualties.	
"	23/4/17		Nothing to report	
"	" 24th		Two guns No 3 Section gave overhead covering fire into OSSUS WOOD (x.29.b central) to support attack by infantry in right sector on SPUR NORTH of the TOMBOIS FARM – VENDHUILE road in F.6.a. Also the flank of the same spur on x.29.d & 30.c. Fire was opened at 4.15 a.m. and 8,500 rounds of ammunition fired. 2/Lieut. B.C.SKEE, O.C. No 1 Section, 126 H.S Coy and ground disturbed the Casualty at F.3 & 7.5.	

2449   Wt. W14957/Mg0 750,000 1/16 J.B.C. & A. Forms/C.2118/12.

Army Form C. 2118.

WAR DIARY
or
INTELLIGENCE SUMMARY.
(Erase heading not required.)

Instructions regarding War Diaries and Intelligence Summaries are contained in F.S. Regs., Part II. and the Staff Manual respectively. Title pages will be prepared in manuscript.

Place	Date 1917.	Hour	Summary of Events and Information	Remarks and references to Appendices
PIEZIERE	25/4/17		Dispositions of Machine Guns in 126" Bde Sector are as follows:— Firing line & Supports. F.5.a.4.5 – X.28.a.15 – X.28.a.08 – X.27.c.9.0 – X.22.c.5½ – X.21.895 – X.21.c.7.5 – X.21.a.2.5. And on right position X.22.c.5.4 – X.25.a.44 – X.25.a.44 – X.25.a.44 – X.25.a.44 – BROWN LINE.– F.8.64 – F.8.46 – F.2.c.82 – F.1.8.62 – F.1.8.53 – F.1.8.1.9 – X.25.a.44 – X.25.a.2.5.	(initials)
PIEZIERE	26/4/17.		Nothing to report.— Two officers reported for duty from Machine Gun Corps Base Depôt CAMIERS. viz. 2/Lieut. CLARK. M.G.C. and 2/Lieut. PRATLEY. M.G.C.	(initials)
"	27/4/17.		Nothing to report.	(initials)
"	28/4/17		Nothing to report.	(initials)
"	29/4/17.		Section No 1. on right of BROWN LINE relieved by Section of 127th Machine Gun Coy at 6 p.m. No 3 Section relieved by right Section of 127 M.G. Coy at 12.20 p.m. These sections proceeded by march route to LONGAVESNES.	(initials)
"	30/4/17		Section No. 2. on left of BROWN LINE relieved by Section of 127th M.G. Coy at 4 p.m. No 4 Section on left of front line relieved by 127 M.G. Coy at 12.30 p.m. Section 1 & 2 proceeded to take up position in the Reserve Line ROISEL – VILLERS FAUCON – SAULCOURT (NEW BLUE) LINE at 5.17 p.m. respectively. Position about E.22.d.6.6; E.23.b.23 & 79.1; C.6T. in night out action E.10.d.51. E.10. C.75; E.10. a. 24; E.10.a.07 in left out action. HQ. Transport S.14 Section in (illegible)	(initials)

Army Form C. 2118.

126 M.G. Coy
Q.S. 54/15.

961 4

WAR DIARY
or
INTELLIGENCE SUMMARY
(Erase heading not required.)

Summary of Events and Information

Confidential

No. 126 MACHINE GUN COY.

Vol. XIV.

Period From 1st May 1917.
To 31st May 1917.

Ref. Maps
62.0. N.E. 1/20,000
57c. S.E.   1/20,000
57 c.N.E.   1/20,000

Instructions regarding War Diaries and Intelligence Summaries are contained in F. S. Regs., Part II. and the Staff Manual respectively. Title Pages will be prepared in manuscript.

Place	Date	Hour

Army Form C. 2118.

WAR DIARY
or
INTELLIGENCE SUMMARY.
(Erase heading not required.)

Instructions regarding War Diaries and Intelligence Summaries are contained in F.S. Regs., Part II. and the Staff Manual respectively. Title pages will be prepared in manuscript.

Place	Date	Hour	Summary of Events and Information	Remarks and references to Appendices
LONGAVESNES	1/5/17		Checking of gun material & equipment.	
"	2/5/17		Whole of NEW BLUE LINE taken over by 126 Bde. Six more machine guns detailed to positions as follows: 2 guns at No 1. Post (K.11.a.51); 2 guns at No. 2 Post (K.5.d.1.2); 2 guns at No 4 Post (E 30.c.1.D).	
	3/5/17		Company baths.	
	4/6/17		Transport Complete.	
	5/5/17		The left front line & the whole of the BROWN LINE taken over from No 3 & 4 distins relieved two sections of 125 m.g. Coy. No 3 at Villers Faucon No 4 at CACHETTE WOOD	
	6/5/17			
	7/5/17			
	8/5/17		TRANSPORT LINES moves to E 28 B.1.5. 2S A 2 use indirect fire on enemy position at Malakoff Farm on the ground N & E	
	9/5/17		A 2 2S used four guns for indirect fire from F 23 A 27 at 10.5 pm on ground North & East of MALAKOFF FARM	
	10/5/17		Guns in Green line moved to following positions No 1 F29 B 3 5 No 2 F 24 B08 F24 A 1 5 F 24 A 1. No 5 F 17 B 8. 1. No 6 F 17 B 8. 3 No 7 F 11 B 6. 3 No 8 F 11 B 4 5. 2 S A 4 on R. Victor. 2nd Lieutenant 9 3rd Lloyd joined from Depot Base. 2S A 2 relieved 2S A 1 in rest. 2S A 3 relieved 2S A 3 into Roussoy. L/cpl Hall killed by fragments of our neighbours shell. Enemy fired 160 shells into Roussoy	
	11/5/17			
	12/5/17		Very quiet day. 1000 rounds M.C. Post a few trees cut at 10.30 pm and appeared to be a building H.S.G.E.	
			C.S.M. TOZER arrived for duty with the Company	
	13/5/17		C.S.M. Brooks left the Coy to report to the Base.	

Army Form C. 2118.
2

WAR DIARY
or
INTELLIGENCE SUMMARY.
(Erase heading not required.)

Instructions regarding War Diaries and Intelligence Summaries are contained in F. S. Regs., Part II. and the Staff Manual respectively. Title pages will be prepared in manuscript.

Place	Date	Hour	Summary of Events and Information	Remarks and references to Appendices
ST EMILIE	14/5/17		Nothing to report	
"	15/5/17		No.1 sector relieved No.2 sector in the left sector of the line at dusk — No.2 sector going into reserve at Coy HQrs	
"	16/5/17		Nothing to report	
"	17/5/17		Company relieved on the line by 4th Cavalry Brigade M.G. Squadron. After relief Company moved into billets at LONGAVESNES	
LONGAVESNES	18/5/17		Cleaning of equipment	
"	19/5/17		Company moved to EQUANCOURT via NURLU and FINS. Went into bivouac.	
EQUANCOURT	20/5/17		Company moved into billets at NEUVILLE	
NEUVILLE	21/5/17		126th M.G.Coy relieve 59th M.G.Coy in the line — Disposition as follows: Three sections in line & one in reserve at Coy HQrs. Q.13.d.4.8. (Sheet 57cSE) — No.2 section to right sector with guns in following positions — Q.11.d.5.6 – Q.10.d.0.11 – Q.17.a.4.6 – Q.17.a.2.6 & Q.11.a.3.3. — No.3 section relieved centre sector with guns at Q.4.d.9.8 – Q.4.b.7.8 – Q.10.a.9.3 & Q.9.c.7.2 – Q.16.a.0.5. — No.1 section relieved left sector with guns at Q.4.c.8.9 – Q.9.b.6.2. No.4 section in reserve also for anti-aircraft duties	
HAVRINCOURT WOOD Q.13.d.4.8	22/5/17		Nothing to report	

Army Form C. 2118.

WAR DIARY
or
INTELLIGENCE SUMMARY.
(Erase heading not required.)

Instructions regarding War Diaries and Intelligence Summaries are contained in F.S. Regs., Part II. and the Staff Manual respectively. Title pages will be prepared in manuscript.

Place	Date	Hour	Summary of Events and Information	Remarks and references to Appendices
HARINCOURT WOOD	23/3/17		Nothing to report	
"	24/3/17		Three Vsu guns fired into FEMY WOOD (Q & 879) with Verbal indirect fire by night. The guns were recorded at Q9.a.4.0 and 3750 rounds S.A. were expended.	
"	25/3/17		—	
"	26/3/17		No 1 section in reserve at Coy HQrs relieved No 4 section in the centre sector of the line. — No 4 section coming into Reserve at Coy HQrs	
"	27/3/17		Nothing to report	
"	28/3/17		Six of our machine guns fired at night on targets from a position Q5e.9.2 a bt the crossroads at R30.d.9.2 reached & RIBECOURT.	
"	29/3/17		Our force of guns from Q9 & cross roads reach traverse road at K31.a.50. & K.29.d.15 from 11 p.m. to 2 midnight.	
"	30/4/17		The following change of disposition section took place at dark. The 1 section in the centre sector of the brigade front relieved the 3 section on the left sector. " 3 " " " " " 1 " " " Left	
"	31/3/17		Nothing to report.	

Commanding 128 M.G. Coy

Army Form C. 2118.

WAR DIARY
INTELLIGENCE SUMMARY
(Erase heading not required.)

Vol 5

Place	Date	Hour	Summary of Events and Information	Remarks and references to Appendices
			No. 126th Machine Gun Coy.	Ref. Maps. 57c S.E. 1/20,000 57c N.E. 1/20,000
			Vol. XV Period 1st June 1917 to 30th June 1917.	

Instructions regarding War Diaries and Intelligence Summaries are contained in F. S. Regs., Part II. and the Staff Manual respectively. Title Pages will be prepared in manuscript.

WAR DIARY or INTELLIGENCE SUMMARY

Army Form C. 2118.

Place	Date	Hour	Summary of Events and Information	Remarks and references to Appendices
HAVRINCOURT WOOD (Q.3.a.4.6)	1/6/17		Four of our guns fired from a position Q9.B.14 on to targets K.28.d.Y.2. and K.34.a.Y.2. The fire was not directed between the hours of 11 p.m 30/5/17 and 1 am 1/6/17 — 15000 rds S.A.A. were expended at dusk Nos 3 + 4 section relieved 1 in regt and north sector of Brigade Front by Nos 1 + 2 M.G. Coy. — At dawn two our Company took up guns in the new Brigade Front. No 1 Section took up gun in Front Support line in position as follows Q.4.c.7.8 Q.4.c.9.4 - Q.4.c.4.9 - Q.9.B.6.2 and No 4 section took up guns in Reserve and intermediate lines in the following positions Q.3.c.6.2 - Q.9.c.7.2 - Q.15.a.7.9 - Q.7.6.1.	EMcN
"	2/6/17		Nothing to report.	EMcN
"	3/6/17		No. 2 Section relieved No 4 section in the reserve line at dark and No 4 section relieved No 1 section in the Front and Support Lines. — No 1 section in reserve at Coy HQrs. — One of our guns fired ranging shots on enemy communication trench from 10 p.m. to 12 mid. on 4/6/17.	EMcN
"	4/6/17		Nothing to report.	EMcN
"	5/6/17		Two section 125 M.G. Coy attached to Company for Barrage purposes. During the night they fired on the gaps in the wire in front of the HINDENBURG LINE	EMcN

WAR DIARY
INTELLIGENCE SUMMARY

Army Form C. 2118.

Place	Date	Hour	Summary of Events and Information	Remarks and references to Appendices
HAVRINCOURT WOOD	6/6/17		Company relieved by 125 M.G. Coy & moved into billets at YPRES. Two sections left under orders of O.C. 125 M.G. Coy for Barrage purposes.	B/MYK
YPRES	7/6/17		Nothing to report. Above two sections relieved by Nos. 1 & 3 sections.	B/MYK
"	8/6/17		Training.	B/MYK
"	9/6/17		Do.	B/MYK
"	10/6/17		Do.	B/MYK
"	11/6/17		Nos. 2 & 4 sections relieve No. 1 & 3 sections attached to 125 M.G. Coy for Barrage purposes. Nos. 1 & 3 move into reserve at Coy HQrs.	B/MYK
"	12/6/17		The following alterations were made in the disposition of the sections: No. 4 section to SANCTUARY "CROAKERS" Regtl Brigade sector left. " 1 " " " " " " " and No. 2 section to remain attached of 125 M.G. Coy for Barrage purposes. No. 3 section in reserve at Company HQrs.	B/MYK

WAR DIARY
or
INTELLIGENCE SUMMARY.
(Erase heading not required.)

Army Form C. 2118.

Place	Date	Hour	Summary of Events and Information	Remarks and references to Appendices
YPRES.	13/6/17		Nothing to report	B/MML
"	14/6/17		A demonstration clearly the effects of chlorine gas out on Vickers Guns & Lewis Guns & well ammunition took place at Bienvillers Wood. The belts were exposed to the gas for about 6 hours and the guns about 2 hours. The guns were afterwards tested. The Vickers gun fired a complete belt with less stoppages and the Lewis gun two magazines with very few stoppages. A further test was carried out with ammunition covered with gas etc. The Vickers gun fired well but the Lewis gun has trouble with the extractor.	B/MML
"	15/6/17		Nothing to report	B/MML
"	16/6/17		No 2 Section relieved by No 3 Section at disposal of O.C. 125th M.G. Coy for Barrage fire.	B/MML
"	17/6/17		Inspection of Transport by Col. Coulson. O.C. Divisional Train. New gun positions constructed in the vicinity of V.36.c.0.4. Second line to cover Left Flank. The following are the coordinates of position in Second Line Q.13.a.7.1; P.18.b.8.5; P.12.a.9.9. R.12.a.4.0. Intermediate Line Q.15.a.5.6; Q.4.b.9.9. Q.8.c.3.8; Q.7.b.7.5.	B/MML

Army Form C. 2118.

WAR DIARY
or
INTELLIGENCE SUMMARY
(Erase heading not required.)

Instructions regarding War Diaries and Intelligence Summaries are contained in F. S. Regs., Part II. and the Staff Manual respectively. Title Pages will be prepared in manuscript.

Place	Date	Hour	Summary of Events and Information	Remarks and references to Appendices
YPRES.	18/6/17		Training	BRWL
"	19/6/17		Training	BRWL
"	20/6/17		Inspection of Cook Houses & Transport Lines by G.O.C.	BRWL
"	21/6/17		Preparation for taking over the night Sector Div. Front. from 125th M.G. Coy. 1 Suicide pen gun. to& round 24 hours in line before the relief.	BRWL
YPRES — HAVRINCOURT WOOD.	22/6/17		Company relieved 125th M.G. Coy. No. 4 Section on night occupying four positions Q.4.d.2.6; Q.4.d.1.6; Q.3.d.4.6, Q.3.d.3.7. Sun 172 firing on bearing 34.5°M; 37.4 on bearing 69°M. No. 3 Section on Left occupying three positions 5, 6, 7. — Q.3.c.4.9. 34.6°M.—76. Q.26.9.6 bearing 52°M. — No 7. Q.2.c.7.6. daylight positions firing into HAVRINCOURT, CHATEAU WOOD K33 & 27 generally. Two Sections, 1 & 2 remain in Reserve at HQrs. Q.13.d.7.8. and used for Indirect overhead firing by night. Section in Second Line & Intermediate Line relieved by 125th M.G. Coy	BRWL
HAVRINCOURT WOOD.	23/6/17	2.30 p.m. 10.35 p.m.	No 2 Section employed Indirect Overhead Fire from position Q.8.b.9.8. between 10.35 p.m. Targets engaged (a) Cross Roads K.34.b.17. (b) Sunken Road. K.27.d.3.0. & K.27.d.5.9. (c) Crossroads at K.28.c.2.5 & near N. end of copse. total rounds fired 6,000. Enemy machine guns replied.	BRWL
"	24/6/17	10.30 – 2.30 a.m.	No.1 Section employed Indirect Overhead Fire from Q.8.b.9.8 between 10.30 – 2.30 a.m. Targets (a) K.26.c.4.7 – K.26.c.0.7 (b) Sunken road from K.34.b.4.9 to K.34.a.0.6. (c) Second road from K.34.c.5.8 to K.34.a.8.2. — Rounds fired 7,000.	BRWL

Army Form C. 2118.

WAR DIARY
or
INTELLIGENCE SUMMARY.
(Erase heading not required.)

Instructions regarding War Diaries and Intelligence Summaries are contained in F. S. Regs., Part II. and the Staff Manual respectively. Title pages will be prepared in manuscript.

Place	Date	Hour	Summary of Events and Information	Remarks and references to Appendices
HAVRINCOURT WOOD	25/6/17	10.30 pm to 2.30 am 26th	Indirect fire guns fired on (a) Harassed line K.27.d.3.2 to K.24.a.6.7 (b) Line K.34.a.3.9 to K.34.b.2.3. (c) Searched road from K.27.d.3.0 to K.27.d.5.9. Rounds fired 6,000 cca.	8RWF
"	26/6/17	10.30 pm to 2.30 am	Indirect Fire on (a) Searched from K.34.b.51. to K.34.a.9.7. (b) Searched Copse in 3Bl. (a) Crew woods at K.28.c.25. Infantry report that m.g. kept down enemy m.g. activity. No. 7 gun (Q.2.0.7.6) disposed of working party in HAVRINCOURT at 3. pm.	8RWF
"	27/6/17	do.	Indirect Fire on (a) Roads K.34.b.51 to K.34.a.9.7. (b) Suspected Battn HQ at K.28.c.4.7 to K.28.c.9.7. (c) Searched main road from K.27.d.3.0 to K.27.d.5.9. Rounds fired 10,000. Enemy M.G.s replied throughout the night.	8RWF
"	28/6/17		Enemy used gas shells on our own Support Line. Two men of No 6 gun team to hospital suffering from gas.	8RWF
"	29/6/17		Intelligence reports German Relief of the 2nd Battn. 36th Fusilier Regt. by the 1st Battn. Took place tonight. Indirect fire guns engaged the following targets:- (a) Roads & Search Parties at K.34.b.2.8. (b) Roads & Copse at K.34.a.2.8. (c) Search Road from K.27.d.3. to K.27.b.5. Rounds fired 5,000. A new daylight position in TRESCAULT completed at 2.A.d.2.6 and indirect fire positions at Q.3.d.4.6 and Q.4.d.3.7.	8RWF
"	30/6/17		Indirect fire on (a) Crossroads K.28.c.25. (b) Searched road from K.27.d.3. to K.27.b.5. Sections 3 & 4 relieved by Sections 1 and 2 respectively.	8RWF

AMWilkshaw Lieut
O/C 126 2/9 By

1/7/17.

Army Form C. 2118.

WAR DIARY
or
INTELLIGENCE SUMMARY.
(Erase heading not required.)

No 126 Machine Gun Coy

Vol XVI

Period 1 July 1917
to
31 July 1917

5 Appendices attached..

Ref. Maps
57 c S.E 1/20,000
57 c N.E 1/20,000
57 c N.W 1/20,000

WAR DIARY
or
INTELLIGENCE SUMMARY.
(Erase heading not required.)

Army Form C. 2118.

Place	Date	Hour	Summary of Events and Information	Remarks and references to Appendices
MAURICOURT WOOD	1/7/17		Sections 3 & 4 relieved by Sections 1 & 2. Mine dugouts commenced at Gun Position 1, 2 and 5. Fatigue party of 16 provided by Company of 12 men provided by Battalion. Work under O.C. 252 Tunnelling Coy R.E.	(5)
Do	2/7/17		Indirect fire on (a) Crossroads at K.34.b.1.7. (b) Copse in K.33.b. (c) Roads & Copse at K.34.a.2.8.	(6)
	3/7/17		Artillery bombardment of FENY WOOD. 6 in M.G.s fired from Q.3.d.6.6 on to FENY WOOD throughout the night.	(7)
	4/7/17		Guns 1 & 2 altered to fire between K.34.c.4.6 & K.34.d.2.4 — Sap in Artillery Barrage. One to Indirect night firing guns at Q.8.b.9.8. given orders to fire on this line on General S.O.S. going up.	(8)
	5/7/17		Guns M.G. fired on (a) Suspected B'n HQs K.28.c.4.7. (b) Searchlight road K.34.c.5.8 & K.30.a.8.2. (c) Crossroads & Copse K.34.a.2.8. between 10.15 pm & 2.30 am.	(9)
	6/7/17		O.C. 78th M.G. Coy taken round the Line. Preparations for relief.	(5)
	7/7/17		Company relieved by 175th M.G. Coy. Moved down to YPRES.	(5)

WAR DIARY
INTELLIGENCE SUMMARY.
(Erase heading not required.)

Army Form C. 2118.

Place	Date	Hour	Summary of Events and Information	Remarks and references to Appendices
YPRES.	8/7/17		Rest & Bathing	
YPRES to BIHUCOURT	9/7/17		Company moved to BIHUCOURT (operation orders attached)	APPENDIX I Operation Order No. 13.
BIHUCOURT	10/7/17		Checking of stores, equipment &c.	APPENDIX II Operation Order No. 14.
	11/7/17		The whole Brigade moved to COURCELLES	
COURCELLES	12/7/17		Baths & preparation of New Camp.	Appendices III
do	13/7/17		Training	
do	14/7/17		Do. T.A.B. inoculation for men not done during last 12 mos.	C
	15/7/17		Cleaning & polishing & equipment.	
	16/7/17		Training	
	17/7/17		Do	
	18/7/17		Do	
	19/7/17		Do	D

WAR DIARY
or
INTELLIGENCE SUMMARY.
(Erase heading not required.)

Army Form C. 2118.

Instructions regarding War Diaries and Intelligence
Summaries are contained in F. S. Regs., Part II.
and the Staff Manual respectively. Title pages
will be prepared in manuscript.

Place	Date	Hour	Summary of Events and Information	Remarks and references to Appendices
Courcelles	1917 July 20		Company Training AB	Appendix IV
	July 21		Company Training	
	July 22		Sunday Divine Service 4 pm C of E. AB	
	July 23		Company training Lecture 4.30 – 5 pm AB	
	July 24		Company Range practices with Machine Guns rifles & revolvers.	
	July 25		Company training	
	July 26		do	AB
	July 27		do Two Officers 2/Lt Thorburn & 2/Lt Peart joined from France.	AB
	July 28		do	AB
	July 29		do	AB
	July 30		do Divisional Sports.	AB
	July 31		do Heats for Brigade Sports. All rifles & revolvers examined by Ordnance. AB	Appendix V

31-7-17

A. J. [signature] Capt
O.C. 126th M.G. Coy.

126 Machine Gun Company

Programme of Training for week ending Wednesday 18th July 1917.

Time	THURSDAY 12th July	FRIDAY 13th July	SATURDAY 14th July	SUNDAY 15th July	MONDAY 16th July	TUESDAY 17th July	WEDNESDAY 18th July
7.0 – 7.45 a.m.	Squad Drill with Arms marching in to numbers. Driving in Revolver Practice	Arms Drill	Guard Mounting		Arms Drill	Squad Drill	Squad Drill
	and anything for men not armed with rifles; Rifles and Revolvers to be exchanged 10 minutes daily – Aiming and rapid loading.						
9.30 a.m. to 12.0.0 a.m.	Inspection Packing Limbers Limber Drill	½ hour Coy Drill Company Drill with Transport. Dress: Drill Order	½ hour Coy Drill Company Drill with Transport Dress: Marching Order	F.P. Inspecting of Equipment and Stocking up Company	Musketry & Fire Part I Table 5 or Rifle & Lewis Gunits (with Transport)	Section Scheme	½ hour Company Drill Company Drill with Transport Coming into action from limbers
2.0 – 3.0 P.M.	General Description and Mechanism	Physical Training	Aiming Instruction Angle of Sight Test		Elementary Gun Drill	Physical Training	Tests of Elementary Training
3.0 – 4.0 P.M.	Belt filling by hand and Machine	N.C.O.s. Communication Drill. men. Immediate action	Stripping		Mechanism	Points before, during and after firing	Immediate Action
5.0 – 5.50 P.M.	Allocation of Duties	Men Range cards and methods of ranging. N.C.O.s Chain of Responsibilities Coy Standing Orders Drill.	Map reading and Compass.		Judging Distance and Visual Training	Battle Action	Machine Gun Intelligence

LECTURES.

N.C.O.s. Lecture ½ hour daily under 2nd in Command and C.S.M. "Interior Economy"

(Signed) E.R.M Kirkpatrick
Major
O.C. 126 Machine Gun Coy.

Appendix

II

Copy No

Operation Orders 14 by
by Major E. R. M. KIRKPATRICK
Comm'g 126th M.G. Coy

d/10/7/17.

1. Company will move to COURCELLES on the morning of July 11 1917

2. The Coy. will march closed up — an interval of 200 yds will be kept between units.

3. There will be no halts during the march

4. Transport will march closed up with units.

5. Brigade HQT. will close here & open at COURCELLES at 10 a.m on 11th inst.

6. Route via GOMMECOURT.

7. The Company will pass

the starting point at 10.34 a.m. Starting Point at present unknown, but Coy. will probably fall in at 10 a.m. & move at 10.15am.

8. Supplies will be drawn at present Refilling Point at 9 a.m. on 11th inst. on Supply Wagons. Supply Wagons will then proceed to New Area in charge of guide to be provided by Units. Transport Officer to arrange for guide.

9. One Motor Lorry has been allotted to Coy. to do two journeys. Lorries will be at Fork Roads G.11.d.8.3 at 8 a.m. & a guide to be sent to this place by this time when they will be allotted by Bde. Transport Officer.

10. Surplus tents & bivouac sheets will be piled

at 2.M.S Stores. One N.C.O & 3 men to be detailed by C.S.M. will remain to load these & will then be marched to New Area under Capt. HYDE 1/9ᵗʰ MAN. R.

11. One officer (2/Lt BARCLAY & 6 men will remain as rear party to remove all manure & fill up all latrines. This party will report to the Field Officer of the Day at present Bde. HQ when their camp is thoroughly clean. They will be marched in one body to COURCELLES.

RM Luke Cathcart
Major

3 copies to O.C. 126ᵗʰ M G Coy
No 1. Filed
2. War Diary
3. Transport Officer

Appendix III

9. Special attention to be paid to March Discipline. Steel helmets will be worn, caps will be carried on the left shoulder, greatcoats rolled on the belt in waterproof sheet. No man is to be allowed to fall out unless he obtains written permission of an officer.

10. Between YTRES & O.16 there will be a 100" interval between Company & Transport. From O.16 to completion of march the Company will march closed up.

11. Billets & horse lines at YTRES are to be left scrupulously clean. Second in Command will stay behind & obtain certificates from TOWN MAJOR as to their cleanliness.

5 Copies
No 1. — filed
2. — 12th Bde.
3. — 2 Lt ANATLEY
4. — Officer i/c Transport
   to be shown to 4.T.O, A.S.C & Coal

O.C. 126th M.G. Coy.
Major
MACRO

5. War Diary.

Appendix.

I.

a halt
made to water, there will be
made at BAPAUME to water &
feed.

6. Haversack rations will be
arranged.

7. 2/Lt PRATLEY S.B. will
arrange to meet the Company
on the BIEFVILLERS - BIHUCOURT
ROAD, at such distance as is
most convenient to guide it to
the new camp.

8. The party at present at
BARASTRE will proceed with
430th Coy. A.S.C. with
remainder of Brigade as ordered.
On arrival of this Company at
their destination, they will
proceed with the supply wagon
carrying the Company rations
for the 10th inst to our camp
in the new area reporting
to 2/Lt PRATLEY.
The N.C.O i/c this party will
take his orders for 9th inst from
O.C. 430th Coy A.S.C.

OPERATION ORDERS No 5
by Major E R M Kirkpatrick
Comm'g 126th Machine Gun Coy.

Reference Sheet 57 C. 1/40,000

8/7/17

1. 126th Machine Gun Coy. will remain at YTRES on the night of 8/9th inst.

2. A loading party of 2 officers and 100 other ranks will be at the Brigade Dump YTRES at 7.30 a.m. to load train & will return to camp on completion.

3. Company will move at 9.30 a.m. to BIHUCOURT G.17. Route BUS — BARASTRE — VILLERS-AU-FLOS — RIENCOURT — BAPAUME — BIEFVILLERS — BIHUCOURT.

Halts — 10 minutes at the Clock Hour and 5 minutes at 30 mins. after the Clock hour.

4. If arrangements can be

APPENDIX IV

126. Machine Gun Company

Programme of Training for week ending Thursday, 26th July 1917

Time	Friday 20th July	Saturday 21st July	Sunday 22nd July	Monday 23rd July	Tuesday 24th July	Wednesday 25th July	Thursday 26th July
9 – 9:45 a.m.	Packing Limbers 10 minutes aiming + loading	Company Drill 10 minutes aiming + loading		Packing Limbers 10 minutes	Rough Ground Drill Revolver Practice	Packing Limbers. Aiming and Loading	Company Drill
9:30 – 12 noon	Company Drill with Limbers	Carrying equipment across country. Action from limbers		Range. Part I Table C. Musketry and Revolver	Range	Range. Part I Table C Musketry and Revolver	Direct and Indirect Laying. Fire Orders
2:0 – 4:0 P.M.	Obtaining direction and elevation by dial and clinometer.	Action from limbers		Immediate Action Gun Drill Combined Drill	Laying out lines of fire by night and Barrage work	Compulsory Sports	Construction of Firing Seats
4:30 – 5:0 P.M.	Lecture on methods of Carrying Gun & equipment across country			Lecture on laying out lines of fire by night, and Barrage work.	Lecture Fire Orders + Construction of Firing Seats		Lecture Consolidation of Shell holes

Note: Arrangements will be made to have Sections on the disposal of the infantry for practising the attack. Runners will be attached, a Course in the mode of Companies on funding enemy scouts/patrols & stars(?) mines. Complaints to be practised separately. Direct firing to be practised by still members at night.

(Signed) E.R.M. Kirkpatrick Major
O.C. 126 Machine Gun Company

APPENDIX V

126th Machine Gun Company

Programme of Training for Week ending 2nd August 1917

Time	Friday 27th July	Saturday 28th July	Sunday 29th July	Monday 30th July	Tuesday 31st July	Wednesday 1st August	Thursday 2nd August
7-7.45 am	Squad Drill with Arms. 10 minutes aiming & loading	Company Drill	Squadding & aiming	Guard mounting. 10 minutes Revolver practice in Aiming & Loading	Packing Limbers	Squad Drill	Company Drill
9.30 - 12 Noon	Company Drill Section Schemes.	Coming into Action from Limbers	Range Firing	Range Firing	Section Schemes	Company Drill Masking of Machine Gun emplacements in Trenches	Range Firing
2.0 - 4 PM	Tests of Elementary Training Physical Training	/	/	Best drilling by hand and by machine. Tests of Elementary Training	Use of Compass. Judging Distance. Calls. Visual Training.	Compulsory Sports.	Immediate Action in Gas masks. Combined Drill
4 - 4.30 PM	Lecture:— Machine Gun Barrage.	/	/	Lecture:— Combined Sights.	Lecture:— Overhead fire	/	Lecture:— Indirect overhead fire

(Signed) Y. Bloor. Capt.
O.C. 126 Machine Gun Coy.

Army Form C. 2118.

WAR DIARY
or
INTELLIGENCE SUMMARY.
(Erase heading not required.)

No. 126. M. G. Coy.

VOL XVII

Period 1st August 1917
to
31st August 1917

Ref. Maps.
57. N.E. 1/20,000.
57. D. 1/40,000.
28. N.W. 1/20,000.

September

WAR DIARY
INTELLIGENCE SUMMARY.
(Erase heading not required.)

Army Form C. 2118.

Place	Date	Hour	Summary of Events and Information	Remarks and references to Appendices
COURCELLES.	1/8/17		Company training	2/Lieut S
-do-	2/8/17		-do-	2/Lieut S
-do-	3/8/17		-do-	2/Lieut S
-do-	4/8/17		-do-	2/Lieut S
-do-	5/8/17		Brigade Church Parade Service. 2nd Lt. K.L. FISHER joined Company, Posted from Base Depot.	2/Lieut S
-do-	6/8/17		Company training.	2/Lieut S
-do-	7/8/17		Brigade Scheme.	2/Lieut Appendix 2.
-do-	8/8/17		Company Training - 2nd Lt Moor proceeded to M.G.T.C. Grantham.	2/Lieut S
-do-	9/8/17		-do-	2/Lieut S
-do-	10/8/17	-	-do-	2/Lieut S
-do-	11/8/17		Brigade Sports.	2/Lieut S

Army Form C. 2118.

WAR DIARY
or
INTELLIGENCE SUMMARY.
(Erase heading not required.)

Instructions regarding War Diaries and Intelligence Summaries are contained in F.S. Regs., Part II. and the Staff Manual respectively. Title pages will be prepared in manuscript.

Place	Date	Hour	Summary of Events and Information	Remarks and references to Appendices
COURCELLES	12/8/17		Church Parade	RAMC
"	13/8/17		Company Training	RAMC
"	14/8/17		Do. Lecture to officers by Divisional Gas Officer	RAMC
"	15/8/17		Company Training	RAMC
"	16/8/17		Do	RAMC
"	17/8/17		Lecture to officers by Divisional Gas Officer	RAMC
"	18/8/17		Company Training	RAMC
"	19/8/17		Church Parade	RAMC
"	20/8/17		Company Training	RAMC
"	21/8/17		Company moved by march route to BEAUCOURT-SUR-ANCRE and entrained for PROVEN (BELGIUM) detraining there about midnight.	RAMC
BERTRANCOURT	22/8/17		Company moved by march route to BERTRANCOURT.	RAMC

Army Form C. 2118.

WAR DIARY
or
INTELLIGENCE SUMMARY.
(Erase heading not required.)

Instructions regarding War Diaries and Intelligence Summaries are contained in F.S. Regs., Part II. and the Staff Manual respectively. Title pages will be prepared in manuscript.

Place	Date	Hour	Summary of Events and Information	Remarks and references to Appendices
WATOU. N. FLANDERS	23/8/17		Marched into billets. K.17.E.2.3. Used 27 N.E. Belgium's Home.	2/MK
"	24/8/17		Training.	2/MK
"	25/8/17		do	2/MK
"	26/8/17		Company training	2/MK
"	27/8/17		do	2/MK
"	28/8/17		1 Officer & 2 N.C.O. proceed to course at 21 Squadron R.F.C. Lecture by Major ??? white.	2/MK
"	29/8/17		One Officer & 4 O.R. proceeded to YPRES SOUTH AREA as advance billeting party.	2/MK
"	30/8/17		Company moved by march route to station POPPERINGE and entrained for YPRES SOUTH AREA.	2/MK
YPRES	31/8/17		—	2/MK

E.W.M[?] Roberts
Major
Comm[?] 126 Lt. Cy. E. Cy.

WAR DIARY

~~INTELLIGENCE SUMMARY.~~
(Erase heading not required.)

Army Form C. 2118.

Nº 126 MACHINE GUN
COMPANY

VOL. XVIII

Period: 1ˢᵗ September 1917
to
30ᵗʰ September 1917.

Ref Maps.

Sheet 28. N.W. BELGIUM 1/20,000
HOOGE TRENCH MAP. 1/10,000
DUNKERQUE. 1.A 1/100,000
27. N.E. & 27. N.W. 1/20,000

Confidential

Army Form C. 2118.

WAR DIARY
INTELLIGENCE SUMMARY.
(Erase heading not required.)

Instructions regarding War Diaries and Intelligence Summaries are contained in F. S. Regs., Part II. and the Staff Manual respectively. Title pages will be prepared in manuscript.

Place	Date	Hour	Summary of Events and Information	Remarks and references to Appendices
YPRES.	1/9/17		Company relieved the 142nd Machine Gun Company in the line, in the sector immediately on the right of the YPRES-ROULERS RAILWAY.	See Appendix I. 8RMGC
YPRES	2/9/17		Transport and detail left behind when the Company moved into the line in accordance with R.S. 135 moved to H.T.9 c. 3.5.	8 RMGC
"	3/9/17		Four barrage guns fired from J.1.C.1.3 on target at ANZAC and Bass Rands J.3.a.8.9. - 4500 rds expended.	8RMGC
"	4/9/17		Four barrage guns fired from J.1.C.1.3 on three targets viz:- D 26.T.7.3 - J3a.2.4 & J.3.a.8.9. - 5000 rounds were expended. - Inter-section reliefs	8RMGC
"	5/9/17		72369 Pte Spencer E. wounded.	8RMGC
"	6/9/17		Section reliefs. - Barrage laid down by eight machine guns from J.1.C.1.3. on lines D.26 d.15.95 to D 26 a.99.42. and D26 a.90.43 & D 26 a.70.85. Searching & traversing slightly. At 7.20 p.m. & 10.50 p.m. S.O.S. signal were sent up & the own m. guns opened fire - 86 belts of ammunition in all were fired	8RMGC

A 5834 Wt. W4973/M687 750,000 8/16 D. D. & L. Ltd. Forms/C.2118/13.

WAR DIARY
or
INTELLIGENCE SUMMARY.
(Erase heading not required.)

Army Form C. 2118.

2

Instructions regarding War Diaries and Intelligence Summaries are contained in F. S. Regs., Part II. and the Staff Manual respectively. Title pages will be prepared in manuscript.

Place	Date	Hour	Summary of Events and Information	Remarks and references to Appendices
YPRES.	7/9/17		Four Lewis guns from 71 C.I.S. sentry on E. VAMPIRE and fire maintained on short bursts for one hour. Total S.A.A. expended from 7am 6/9/17 to 7am 7/9/17 = 57,250 rounds. Section reliefs.	APPENDIX IV (7)/9/17
"	8/9/17		Our machine guns fired between 10 pm & 4 am on ZONNEBEKE REDOUBT and ANZAC. 4000 rds being expended	8/9/17
"	9/9/17		Emplacement destroyed by S.9 shell & gun buried. No damage to equipment.	9/9/17
"	10/9/17		—	5/9/17
"	11/9/17		Our machine gun opened fire on the S.O.S. going up in KINKS WOOD towards our wire expending about 4000 rounds.	Appendix VII 9/17
"	12/9/17		Section reliefs. See appendix.	Appendix VIII cont.

A5834 Wt. W4973/M687 750,000 8/16 D. D. & L. Ltd. Forms/C.2118/13.

WAR DIARY
or
INTELLIGENCE SUMMARY.

(Erase heading not required.)

Army Form C. 2118.

2

Instructions regarding War Diaries and Intelligence Summaries are contained in F. S. Regs., Part II. and the Staff Manual respectively. Title pages will be prepared in manuscript.

Place	Date	Hour	Summary of Events and Information	Remarks and references to Appendices
YPRES.	13/9/17	—		WMM
"	14/9/17		Inter sector relief.	WMM
"	15/9/17		He now covered by aeroplane bomb.	WMM
"	16/9/17		Company relieved by in the line by 27th M.G. Coy. after relief company moved to B Camp BRANDHOEK (G.6.d.4.5.)	WMM
BRANDHOEK	17/9/17	—		WMM
"	18/9/17		Company training.	WMM
"	19/9/17		Company moved by march route to WINNEZEELE	Appendix II / Appendix III
WINNIZEELE	20/9/17		" do do to WORMHOUDT	Appendix IV
WINNEZEELE	21/9/17			Appendix VI

Army Form C. 2118.

WAR DIARY
or
INTELLIGENCE SUMMARY.
(Erase heading not required.)

Instructions regarding War Diaries and Intelligence Summaries are contained in F. S. Regs., Part II. and the Staff Manual respectively. Title pages will be prepared in manuscript.

Place	Date	Hour	Summary of Events and Information	Remarks and references to Appendices
WORMHOUDT	22/9/17	-	Company moved by march route to ZUYDCOOTE	
ZUYDCOOTE	23/9/17	-	Company moved by march route to LA PANNE (Belgium)	
LA PANNE	24/9/17	-	do do to Surrey Camp (R.32.c.F.6) Relieved 203rd M.G. Coy. 2/LIEUT. CLUBB arrived from Base Depot	Appendix III
SURREY CAMP	25/9/17	-	on Coast Defence	
"	26/9/17		No. 2 Section under LT REYNOLDS attached to 127th Inf Bde	
"	27/9/17		Later section relief - LT. MOFFAT, 2/T. TRAMPLETON and 8 O.R. arrived as reinforcement from M.G.C. Base Depot	
"	28/9/17		-	
"	29/9/17		Later section relief - LT BARCLAY and 5 O.R. arrived as reinforcements from M.G.C. Base Depot.	
"	30/9/17	-	nil. Casualties. 2 OR killed, 1 OR wounded	RSM Will Ratcliffe Major O.C. 126th M.G.C.

126 MACHINE GUN COMPANY ORDER No.16.   Copy No... 6
— BY —
MAJOR E.R.K. KIRKPATRICK.   1/9/17.

The 126th Machine Gun Company will relieve the 142nd Machine Gun Company in the line to-night.

Nos 2 & 4 Sections will relieve the guns in the line and No. 1 Section will take over the Barrage Guns.

No. 3.Section will remain in reserve at the Transport Lines.

Guides will meet the above Sections at the BURR CROSS Roads (I.17.b.3.8.) at the following times :-
   No. 1. Section at 7.0.pm.
   No. 2. Section at 7.15."
   Nos 4. Section at 7.30."
Distances of 50 yards will be maintained between limbers.

The Iron Ration and two complete days rations will be taken by all ranks, also water for one day. The second day's water will be dumped at the BURR CROSS Roads about 7.0.pm. and collected by Section carriers. The brakesmen in charge of limbers will report to Company H.Qrs. when the water and rations arrive. The limbers will not wait but proceed back immediately to Transport Lines.

Company Headquarters will be at RAILWAY WOOD (I.11.b.6.3.) and will accomodate :-
   2 Officers in........A. Dug-out.
   Officers Cookhouse
   & 2 Men.............B. "

   C.S.M. Orderly Room
   Clerk, 3 Signallers
   and 3 extra men......D. "

   3. Runners...........C. "

All returns and correspondence from Sections will be sent to Company Headquarters in RAILWAY WOOD.

All Trench and Area Stores will be taken over and receipts given, copies of which are to be sent to Company Headquarters with the "Relief Complete" report.

Each Section will detail one runner to live at Coy H.Qrs. (I.11.b.6.3.), and Cpl. Walker will detail one signaller to live at Company Transport Lines, to maintain communication with Company Headquarters.
 All runners, ration parties, etc., are to be warned to keep clear of the "Duck Walks" to move quickly across Hell Fire Corner where they are in view of the enemy. Runners are to be used as sparingly as possible.
 Large dumps of machine gun ammunition exist and on no account are Sections to allow these dumps to be interfered with, except in case of emergency, as they are there for a definate purpose.
 The Officer in charge of Barrage Guns is responsible that he receives and understands all previos instructions re the Barrage from the outgoing officer re S.O.S. etc.

Completion of all reliefs will be notified to Company Headquarters by wire and runner, using the Brigade Code.

Copy No 1 – OC W
  2 – X
  3 – Y
  4 – Z
  5 – File
  6 – War Diary
  7 – War Diary
  8 – H.Qrs.

(Sgd). J.F. BLEAKLEY,
Lieut for Major.
Commanding 126 Machine Gun Company.

Appendix. No 2

OPERATION ORDER BY
Major E.R.M. Kirkpatrick.
Commanding 126 Machine Gun Company.

3/86.
Copy No. 5

7th. Sept. 1917.

1. Reference relief to-night.
    Relief will proceed as arranged with the exception that Lt. Reynolds with W. Section will not proceed to Transport Lines but will remain at Company H.Qrs. bringing from Barrage position in KIRKS WOOD the Guns and Equipment of Z Section.

2. During the afternoon of the 8th. Lieut Reynolds with the Personnel of W. Section will proceed to Company Transport Lines to RAILWAY WOOD where they will be accommodated until they are moved up to Barrage position in KIRKS WOOD.

3. Four Guns and Equipment will always remain at Company H.Qrs. in RAILWAY WOOD under the charge of the C.S.M. and will be kept clean by the Section in rest at RAILWAY WOOD. This will be the routine for Section reliefs in future.

4. The scratch detachment will be relieved every fourth night commencing on the night of the 8/9th inst. It will arrive at Company Dug-out on the afternoon of the day of relief, will be sent up to the barrage guns early and will relieve as early as possible.

5. With reference to Section coming into reserve their rations and water will be sent to Coy H.Qrs. in RAILWAY WOOD where if possible tea will be prepared for them on there return from the line, C.S.M. to arrange. At present there is only accommodation for 20 O.Rs. including N.C.Os. & 1 Officer's Batman in addition to personnel of Coy H.Qrs. The 2nd in Command will arrange that that one of the twenty is a cook and that two dixies are sent up.

6. No limbers will be required for relief to-night.

(Sgd). E.R.M. KIRKPATRICK.

Major,

Commanding 126 M.G.Coy.

8/8/17.

Copy No. 1 - OC W
      - 2 - X
      - 3 - Z
      - 4 - Canteacy
      - 5 - Do.
      - 6 - file

Appendix No. III

SECRET. OPERATION ORDERS BY   Copy No. 5
         MAJOR E.R.M. KIRKPATRICK.   5/118.
         Commanding 126 MACHINE GUN COMPANY.

1.   On the night of the 11/12th an attack will be made
on strong point at D.26.c.12.30. herein after referred
to as the HUT. There will be no Artillery preparations
A Special S.O.S. consisting of three green very lights
fired from SEXTON HOUSE will be the signal for four
guns at KIRKS WOOD to open fire in front of ZONNEBEKE
REDOUBT. If the General S.O.S. goes up ordinary S.O.S.
Action will be taken.
     The four guns at KIRKS WOOD will only fire for
seven minutes and only in case the three very lights go up
     O.C. Z. Section will obtain further details from
O.C. JUICE.

     Acknowledge by wire.

Copy No. 1. O.C. X. Section.
  "   " 2. O.C. Z. Section.
  "   " 3. O.C. Rear H.Qrs.
  "   " 4. File.
  "   " 5. War Diary.
          6.

                              (Sgd) J.E. REYNOLDS.
11/9/17.
                                  Lieut for Major.
                              Comndg. JUMP.

OPERATION ORDERS No. 11.   6/6/.
By Major E.R.M. KIRKPATRICK.
Commanding 126 Machine Gun Company.

1. The following relief will take place on the 12th inst.

2. Z. Section will be relieved in the front line by X. Section. Section Officers to make their own arrangements. On completion of reliefs Z. Section will proceed to railway wood where they will remain one night and then proceed to Transport Lines.

3. W. Section will proceed from RAILWAY WOOD to Barrage positions taking over guns and equipment from X. Section.

4. Report relief by wire.

5. Acknowledge.

6. Surplus kit at Barrage position to be carried down from there by Z. Section.

Copies to O.C. X. Section.
   "   " O.C. Z. Section.
   "   " O.C. Rear H.Qrs.
   "   File.

(Sgd). J.E. REYNOLDS.

Lieut for Major.

12/9/17.   Comndg 126 M.G. Coy.

Appendix No V

Appendix No. IV

ORDERS FOR MOVE BY
Major E.R.M. Kirkpatrick.
Commanding 126 Machine Gun Company.

Order No. 16.

20/9/17.

Ref Map 27.-1/40,000.

1. The Company will move to WORMHOUDT AREA on the 21st.

2. Route will be by CROSS Roads J.21.b.5.7.

3. Starting Point Road Junction J.16.b.2.6.

4. Transport will move as one unit and will pass the starting point as follows :-

    1/9th. Manchester Regt.   9.16 am.
    126 Machine Gun Company.   9.21. "
    428 Field Coy. R.E.   9.26. "

5. A gap of 200 yards will be maintained between transport of Units and 20 yds between each group of six vehicles.

6. Personnel will pass starting point as follows :-

    1/9th Manchester Regt.   10.31. am.
    126 Machine Gun Company.)
    126 L. T. M. B.) 10.41. "
    428 Field Coy.) 10.49. "
    1/2. Field Amb.)

7. 500 yards distances will be maintaine between units.

8. Refilling on 21st will be at WINNEZEELE and on 22nd at WORMHOUDT. Supplies for 22nd will be drawn from 430th Coy A.S.C. at new area on arrival.

9. Motor Lorry allotted to 126 L.T.M.B. after unloading will return and convey baggage of 126 M.G.Coy to WORMHOUDT. One N.C.O. will meet this lorry at 8.0. am. tomorrow at J.17.b.3.9. proceed with the Trench Mortars baggage to new area and after unloading guide lorry back to Company H.Qrs.

10. ADVANCE PARTY. An advance party consisting of 2/Lieut Shortridge and 2 N.C.Os. will meet the Staff Captain at AREA COMMANDANTS OFFICE WORMHOUDT. at 8.0.am to-morrow the 21st inst. Distance about six mile. The party will be mounted on bicycles.
The Party will be shown their billeting area and will arrange for guide to meet Company on its arrival.

11. Certificate of Cleanliness will be obtained by rear party consisting of Lieut Bleakley, one N.C.O. to be detailed by Orderly Sergeant.

12. Company will fall in at 10.0. am. ready to move off at 10.10. am. DRESS. Fighting Order. Packs to be carried on Limbers.

13. Transport leaves camp at 8.55. am.

14. Breakfast 7.0. am.

15. Officers valices, mens packs etc., to be dumped ready for loading by 8.15 am. and all limbers to be packed by 8.30 am. with all stores travelling with limbers.

(Sgd) E.R.M. KIRKPATRICK.
Major.
Comndg 126 M.G.Coy.

20/9/17.

Order No 15.

ORDERS FOR MOVE
BY
Major E.R.M. Kirkpatrick.
Commanding 126 Machine Gun Company.

18/9/17.

Ref Maps 27. N.E.) 1
27. N.W.) 20000.

The Company will move by march route tomorrow the 19th Sept. to WINNEZEELE AREA No.1.

Fall in 5.5. am . Ready to move off 5.15 am.

DRESS. Full Marching Order. Waterproff Sheets and Sandbags carried on the belt.

Starting Point will be the CROSS Roads G.5.c. .2.

Personnel of the 126th Infantry Brigade will pass the starting point at the following times :-

Brigade Headquarters	8.10. am.
126. M.G.Coy	8.11. "
1/5th. E. Lancs Regt	8.16. "
1/4th. " "	8.21. "
1/10th. Manchester Regt	8.26. "
1/9th. Manchester Regt	8.31. "

A gap of 200 yards will be left between the Transport of Units and a gap of 20 yards between each group of six vehicles.
The Transport of 126 Brigade Headquarters and 126 Machine Gun Company will march as one unit.
One N.C.O.(to be detailed by the C.S.M.) will march in rear of the 126th Brigade Personnel to collect any men of the Company who fall out(but not admitted by the M.O. to an Ambulance wagon), and march them in a formed body to the destination.

REAR PARTY. A rear party consisting of Lieut Bleakley, one N.C.O. and 3 men(to be detailed by the C.S.M.) will remain behind to finally clean the Camp and obtain certificates for cleanliness of of billets. This party will also act as a loading party, proceed with the Motor Lorry and be responsible for guarding the stores till relieved.

BAGGAGE. Officers valises, mens packs, cooks gear and Officers Mess goods must be packed in limbers by 5.45 am.

SURPLUS BAGGAGE. All surplus baggage and stores to be stacked C.Q.M.S. stores ready for loading on Motor Lorry before the Company moves off.

BILLETS. Section Commanders are responsible that the billets occupied by Sections are left in a clean and sanitary condition.

RATIONS. The unexpended portion of the days ration will be carried on the man.

WATER CART. The water cart and all petrol tins must travel full.

BILLETING AREA. The new billeting area is J.11.a.5.9.

(Sg). J.F. BLEAKLEY.

Lieut for Major.

18/9/17.   Commanding 126 Machine Gun Coy.

Appendix No. VI

Appendix No. VII

ORDERS FOR MOVE BY
Major E.R.M. Kirkpatrick.
Commanding 126 MACHINE GUN COMPANY.

Order No. 19.

23/9/17.

Ref Maps.......

1. The Company less 2 Guns of W. Section will move by March Route to-morrow to SURREY CAMP. (R.32.c.2.7.)

2.   Reveille............ 4.30. am.
      Breakfast........... 5.30. "

3. Fall in 6.30 am ready to move off 6.45. am.

4. DRESS. Full Marching Order - Packs will be worn.

5. TRANSPORT. Limbers for the Sub-Section of W. Section will remain behind and act under the orders of 2/Lieut Fisher who will be in command of this Sub-Section, otherwise transport move with Company.
On arrival at New Camp limbers will be emptied as necessary and transport will return under Lieut Hampson and clear C.Q.M.Sgts dump.

6. Guns, Equipment, Officers valices for the remaining Sub-Section of W. Section will be taken by Pack Transport to their Post.

7. REAR PARTY. A Rear Party consisting of a Sub-Section W.Section and 1 N.C.O. and 9 men to be detailed by C.S.M. will remain behind to load baggage and finally clean billets and obtain certificates for cleanliness of same.

8. Section Commanders are responsible that the billets occupied by their Section are left in a clean and sanitary condition and that no Goverment Stores have been left behind.

9. Limbers will be packed complete by 6.15 am. Any spare space in the limbers will be made up from the C.Q.M.S. dump.

10. DISTRIBUTION. H.Qrs. X. & Y Sections and Transport will be stationed at R.32.c.2.7. Two guns W. Section under under 2/Lieut Fisher will be stationed at W.10.b.3.7. under Lieut Reynolds.
Two guns of Z Section will be stationed at R.32.a.3.7. under Lieut Kelly, this Officer will live at Company Headquarters and Command X & Y Sections.
Two guns of Z. Section will be stationed at R.23.b.0.8. under 2/Lt. Shortridge.
These Posts will be numbered 4.3.2. & 1 in the above order.
Each Posts will consist of one Officer, two N.C.Os and 12 O.Rs.
No 3 Posts will be commanded by a Sergant when the Officer is away.
All necessary gun gear including spare parts boxes to be taken to Posts and 10 Belt boxes per gun.
Section Commanders W. & Z Section will arrange that a senior N.C.O. is left in command of the details at Company Headquarters and in charge of their equipment. Packs will be taken to the Posts.

ORDERS. Orders for Posts are at each post. All maps, orders, and trench stores will be taken over and receipts given by the Officer concerned, forwarding lists to Company Headquarters immediately on completion.

S.A.A. On no account are Officers in charge Posts to allow their S.A.A. to fall below 4 boxes bulk per post.

ANTI-AIRCRAFT SIGHTS. Anti-aircraft sights will be issued as soon as received.

RATIONS. Rations will be delivered daily to Posts by Pack Animals.
Each Post will have 4 Petrol tins - these must be kept filled under local arrangements.

INTELLIGENCE REPORTS.   Intelligence reports until further orders will reach Company Headquarters by 7.30. am daily.

PASSES.   On no account will Post Commanders give passes at any one time to more than 25% of their garrison. Passes must be written, and men leaving must be properly dressed, Box Respirators or P.H. Helmet, Belt, Cap and Badge.

If a Section Officer wishes to leave his Post he will on no account do so unless a Sergeant is present to act for him, in which case he will hand over all instructions etc.

Post Commanders are responsible for the cleanliness of their posts and that their men are properly dressed and clean.

O.C. Posts will arrange for one runner to live at Company Headquarters. These runners will be under the personal charge of the C.S.M.

SIGNALLING.   Cpl Walker will arrange to take over standing wire and signals from Company to be relieved and will hand over equivalent, obtaining a receipt.

WATER.   Drinking Water at Camp. Horse troughs at Camp. All trans- to Posts by Pack Transport from Company Headquarters.

HANDING OVER AND TAKING OVER.   2/Lt. Fisher will arrange for an N.C.O. to be at the KURSAAL HOTEL at 7.30. am to meet an Officer of the 203 Machine Gun Company. This Officer will take over present Camp and will then take 2/Lt. Fisher with his Sub-Section to No.4 Post.

2/Lieut Fisher taking as much of his gun gear on Pack Transport as possible and carrying the remainder. His personnel to make two journeys if necessary. His Transport will then proceed to new Camp via W.23.a.-Cross Roads W.18.c.5.7. - W.6.central to Company H.Qrs. A cyclist guide will be sent back to meet him along this road.

Relief to be reported by the runner sent to Company Headquarters as early as possible. This runner will bring list of Trench Stores with him.

(Sgd). E.R.M. KIRKPATRICK.

Major.

Commanding 126 Machine Gun Company.

Army Form C. 2118.

WAR DIARY
—or—
INTELLIGENCE SUMMARY.
(Erase heading not required.)

Vol 9

No. 126 MACHINE GUN COMPANY

VOL XIX.

Period. 1 October 1917
to
31st October 1917.

R.J. Major

FURNES 1/40000 Provisional Issue
COXYDE 1/20000. Edition 1.
NIEUPORT SECTOR 1/10000 French
{ Map No. 5 - 3rd Edition

Army Form C. 2118.

WAR DIARY
INTELLIGENCE SUMMARY.
(Erase heading not required.)

Instructions regarding War Diaries and Intelligence Summaries are contained in F. S. Regs., Part II. and the Staff Manual respectively. Title pages will be prepared in manuscript.

Place	Date	Hour	Summary of Events and Information	Remarks and references to Appendices
SURREY CAMP. R.32 c.5.6.	1/10/17	—	Training.	
"	2/10/17	—	Inter section relief.	Appendix I
"	3/10/17	—	Training and action at Company HQrs. — Inter section relief.	II
"	4/10/17	—	Do	
"	5/10/17	—	Do	
"	6/10/17	—	126 M.G. Coy. relieved by 124th M.G. Coy. on Coastdefence. After relief Company moved by timed route to COXYDE.	Appendix III
COXYDE	7/10/17	—	126 M.G. Coy. relieved the 14th Machine Gun Company on the ST GEORGES SECTOR of the line. NIEUPORT. at dusk.	Appendix IV
NIEUPORT.	8/10/17	—	Two four machine guns fired 6000 rds. during the night - Overhead indirect fire on 6. M.18.c.90.00. & M.18.c.95.70	

WAR DIARY

INTELLIGENCE SUMMARY.

(Erase heading not required.)

Army Form C. 2118.

(2)

Instructions regarding War Diaries and Intelligence Summaries are contained in F. S. Regs., Part II. and the Staff Manual respectively. Title pages will be prepared in manuscript.

Place	Date	Hour	Summary of Events and Information	Remarks and references to Appendices
NIEUPORT.	9/10/17	—	Our machine guns fired during the night on the following targets:- 1. Track M.24.a 10.30 to M.24.a 30.60. 2. BEETROOT DRAIN from M.24.a 80.20 to M.24.c 65.90 3. Road thro' N.20.a 4. BRUGES ROAD from N.27.d 70.60 to N.33.c. 40.50. 6000 rds S.A.A. were expended	
"	10/10/17.		Our machine guns fired during the night from M.26.a 39.47 on tracks in N.20.c. Expending 4500 rounds.	
"	11/10/17.		do. do. on to target in N.20.c. — T2.d 50.95 + N.27.c. Expending. 4500 rounds.	
"	12/10/17.		Two Heavy machine guns fired from M.36.a 39.47 on to KETSBRUG N.19.c. also on to TRACKS around N.32.b. and ROAD JUNCTION N.27.a 20.15. Expending 6000 rounds.	
"	13/10/17.		Re-distribution of guns. ..... See Appendix V M. Gun firing during night on to N.19.c. - expending 2000 rounds.	Appendix V

Army Form C. 2118.

WAR DIARY
or
INTELLIGENCE SUMMARY.
(Erase heading not required.)

Place	Date	Hour	Summary of Events and Information	Remarks and references to Appendices
NIEUPORT.	14/10/17		Guns reaching from M.26.a 39.47 on target M.24.a 10.30 traversing to M.24.a 20.60. and also on H.18.c 95.40. Expending 5000 rounds. Casualties. 1 O.R. Killed by shell frag.	Appendix VI
"	15/10/17	-	Inter section relief.	
"	16/10/17	-	One section 127" Machine Gun Coy attached to the Company and relieved Z section. During the night two of our guns fired 3000 rounds on KETSBROG N.19.f and TRACKS about RUSSIA POST N.20.c.	Appendix VII
"	17/10/17	-	Inter section relief. 1 O.R. wounded shellfire.	Appendix VIII
"	18/10/17	-	1 O.R. wounded shellfire.	
"	19/10/17		Three sections 12th Welsh M.G. Bn Hqs & one section 11th M.G. Coy attached for Tactical purposes to Company. - Y section relieved sections in all transport lines. The 11th & 12th M.G. Bn Hqs took over positions B.1 & B.3 as the following	Appendix IX

(4) Army Form C. 2118.

WAR DIARY
INTELLIGENCE SUMMARY.
(Erase heading not required.)

Place	Date	Hour	Summary of Events and Information	Remarks and references to Appendices
NIEUPORT			B.1 ———— M.36a 40.27 B.2 ———— M.36a 23.37 B.3 ———— M.36a 15.37 B.4 ———— M.36a 08.37 B.5 ———— M.36a 02.37 B.6 ———— M.35b 94.38 B.7 ———— M.35b 88.39 B.8 ———— M.35b 84.39 These guns are organized as a Battery. Each two guns are commanded by two Officers who are in telephone communication with Company HQrs. See Appendix X.	
"	20/10/17		Two of our guns shelled sword cell during the night on targets M.18a 96.30 and M.17a 95.65. - Harassing fire	Appendix X
"	21/10/17		Appendix X.	Appendix X
"	22/10/17		—	

Army Form C. 2118.

WAR DIARY
or
INTELLIGENCE SUMMARY.
(Erase heading not required.)

Instructions regarding War Diaries and Intelligence Summaries are contained in F.S. Regs., Part II. and the Staff Manual respectively. Title pages will be prepared in manuscript.

Place	Date	Hour	Summary of Events and Information	Remarks and references to Appendices
NIEUPORT	22/10/17		W Section fired 4000 rounds from M29 D.08.00. on KETSBRUG N19.B. 30.75 during the night	
	23/10/17		do 3000 rounds do	
	24/10/17		do 2000 rounds do	
			X Section fired from N31.A.01 on DAM in T.2.D 10,000 rounds expended during the night by orders of D.M.G.O.	APPENDIX XI
	25/10/17		Z Section relieved X Section in the line on the right sector at dusk	
			W Section fired from M29 D.08.00 on BEETROOT DRAIN M29.B. and CROSS ROADS M19.D	
			2000 rounds were expended. Z Section fired on DAM in T.2.D during the night 12,000 rounds were expended	
	26/10/17		W Section fired from M29 D.08.00 on RIVER LANE N19.D and KETSBRUG N19.B 2000 rounds were expended	
	27/10/17		Y Section relieved W Section on the LEFT SECTOR at dusk	APPENDIX XII
			Y Section fired from M29 D.08.00 on BEETROOT DRAIN M24.B and BAMBURGH LANE M19.C	
			3000 rounds were expended	
	28/10/17		—	
	29/10/17		—	
	30/10/17		Major E.R.M. KIRKPATRICK sick to hospital	
	31/10/17		X Section relieved 6 guns of 12th M.M.G. Battery in the line	APPENDIX XIII
				McClung Lt 120MG Coy

Copy No. 6.

126 MACHINE GUN COMPANY ORDER No.25.

1/10/17.

1. The following relief will be carried out tomorrow 2nd October, 1917. about noon.

2. W. Section will relieve Y Section in Nos. 3 & 4 Posts on the Coast Defence.

3. All equipment will be taken over by relieving Section and all receipts for Trench Stores forwarding to Company Headquarters.

4. After relief Y Section will proceed to Company Headquarters.

5. Completion of Relief to be reported to Company H.Qrs by wire and runner.

6. The strength of the Garrison is 12 O.R. including batman and runner.

7. All details of Returns to be rendered, instructions for gun position, points on firing at aircraft and bathing facilities etc., to be handed over to relieving detachments.

8. The Officer Commanding No.3. Post will remain at his post and take command of the relieving detachments, being attached temporarily to W. Section for this purpose.

(Sgd) E.R.M. KIRKPATRICK.
Major.
Commanding 126 M.G.Coy.

Copy No. 1 to O.C. W. Section.
" " 2. to " Y. Section.
" " 3. "   " No. 3 Post.
" " 4. File.
" " 5. War Diary.
" " 6. "   "

APPENDIX. II

126 MACHINE GUN COMPANY ORDER No. 26.

Copy No. 5.

Ref Map........   3/10/17.

1. The following relief will be carried out tonight (3/10/17) about 8.30. p.m.

2. Y Section will relieve Z Section in the line.

3. Relief will proceed with Ration Limbers leaving Company Headquarters about 7.30. p.m. and report to Z Section Headquarters (M.21.d.50.15).

4. The Section will be attached to 127 Brigade.

5. Y Section will move up with two days rations and will not draw again till the night of the 5th inst.

6. Guides to meet ration limbers will be sent to the CROSS ROADS (X.4.c.25.83.) OOST DUNKERQUE arriving there 8.15 p.m.

7. All information regarding guns, water, telephone communication etc., will be handed over to O.C. relieving Section.

8. All equipment will be handed over to relieving Section except guns.

9. O.C. Z Section will notify 127th Brigade of relief.

10. Completion of relief will be reported to 127th Brigade Advanced Headquarters and to 126 Machine Gun Company by wire and runner.

11. RETURNS. All returns will be rendered to 127 Brigade except ration strength and any returns affecting the administration of the Company which will be sent to this Company Headquarters.

12. O.C. Y Section will instruct the four No.1s. of his Section to proceed this afternoon to the positions they are taking over and obtain all information.

13. A Runner will be detailed to remain at Company Headquarters for delivering messages to Section Headquarters.

Copy No.1 to O.C. Y. Section.
 "   " 2. " O.C. Z. Section.
 "   " 3.   File.
 "   " 4.   War Diary.
 "   " 5.   "   "

(Sgd) E.R.M. KIRKPATRICK.
Major.
Commanding
126 Machine Gun Company.

APPENDIX III

126 MACHINE GUN COMPANY.   App. III   Copy No. 6.

ORDER NO. 27.

5/10/17.

Ref Maps COXYDE 1/20,000 Edt 1.

1. **RELIEF.** The 126 Machine Gun Company will be relieved by the 124 Machine Gun Company on Coast Defence about 8.0.a.m. tomorrow 6/10/17.

2. **EQUIPMENT.** All gun equipment will be moved from the positions including tracer ammunition.

3. **TRENCH STORES.** With the above exception all trench stores will be handed over as per lists sent to posts yesterday and receipts forwarded to Company Headquarters.

   All detachments after relief will proceed to Company Headquarters.

4. **GUIDES.** The Officers commanding Posts 3 & 4 will arrange for guides to be at HOTEL KURSAAL LA PANNE at 7.0.a.m. tomorrow to meet and guide their reliefs to the position.

5. **TRANSPORT.** Limbers for 3 & 4 Posts will arrive at the positions at 8.0. a.m. and pack mules for No.1 post at 9.30. a.m. All gun equipment from No.2 post will be man handled to Company Headquarters.

6. **RATIONS.** The extra days ration issued will be brought out of the line, also all Petrol tins, dixies etc.

   Completion of relief to be reported to Company Headquarters.

7. **MOVE.** After concentration at Company Headquarters the Company will move by March Route to COXYDE.

8. **BAGGAGE.** All baggage, Q.M.S. Stores, Orderly Room papers etc., to be stacked outside C.Q.M.Sgts Store by 11.0 a.m. and a guard of 1 N.C.O. & 2 men over same.

9. **BLANKETS.** Blankets will be folded and placed under the valice cover.
   Packs will be carried by the man.

10. **REAR PARTY.** A rear party consisting of one N.C.O. and 4 men (to be detailed by the C.S.M.) will remain behind to finally clean Camp and obtain Certificates for cleanliness of same.

    The water cart and all petrol tins must travel full.

    The unexpended portion of the days ration will be carried on the man.

Copy No. 1. to No. 1. Post.
" " 2. " " 2. "
" " 3. " " 3. "
" " 4. " " 4. "
" " 5. " O.C. Transport.
" " 6. " War Diary.
" " 7. " "   "

E.M.Kirkpatrick

Major.
Commanding 126 Machine Gun Company.

APPENDIX. IV

SECRET.

186 MACHINE GUN COMPANY. ORDER No. 20.

Copy No. 7.

Ref Maps. FURNES 1/40,000 Prov Issue.
Trench Map No. 8. 3rd Edition.
NIEUPORT Sector.

5/10/17.

1. The 186 Machine Gun Company will relieve the 14th Machine Gun Company in the St. Georges Sector on the night of the 7/8 October, 1917.

2. 2/Lieut Fisher with X Section will take over Guns Nos 1.2. 3.4. & No.1 A.A. gun.

3. Lieut Kelly with Y Section will take over guns Nos.5.6.7. & 8. And No.2. A.A. gun.

4. 2/Lieut Barclay with W Section will take over Guns Nos. 9. 10. 11. & 12. and No.3. A.A. gun.

5. Lieut Ramsbottom with Z Section will take over Guns Nos. 13. 14. 15. & 16. and No. 4. A.A. gun.
   Lieut Ramsbottom will live with Guns Nos.13.& 14. and Nos.15. & 16. and A.A. Gun No. 4 will be supervised by the second in command.

6. The above Officers with 1. N.C.O. or man for each gun, 2 Signallers and the C.S.M. will be at the Cross Roads at COXY DUNKERQUE (X.4.d.2.7.) at 10.0. a.m. on the 7th inst. Where arrangements have been made for a guide from 14th M.G.Coy Transport to meet them and conduct them to No 14 M.G.Coy H.Qrs. This party will not proceed as one party but in two's at 100 yards distance.

7. Headquarters No. 14 Machine Gun Company are at M.24.c.8.6.

8. The Company will move from COXYDE to COXY DUNKERQUE on the 7th Inst. at a time to be notified later. The Company will proceed to the line by Sections in the order X.Y.W.& Z - 200 yards between Sections. W. Section will pass the starting point at Cross Roads (X.4.d.2.7.) at 4.30. pm. Where 14th M.G.Coy has arranged guide to meet them. They will proceed under his guidance to M.34.c.9.1. where they will meet an Officer of 14th M.G.Coy who will inform them whether they will empty their limbers there and man handle the gear forward or whether it is safe for the limbers to go forward. In any case O.C. Guns (1.2.3.4.) (5.6.7.8.) (9.10.11.12.) and (13.14)(5. & 16.) will arrange guides for their groups either from No.14 M.G.Coy. or from their own advance party, to be with the Officer at M.34.c.9.1. to guide their sections to their positions.

9. Headquarters limber with Signalling Stores, Orderly Room papers and Officers mess goods will travel in rear of Z Section.

10. Belt boxes will be taken over at positions approximately 14 per gun. Spare part boxes will not be taken beyond Section Headquarters.

11. Blankets will not be taken into the line.

12. DRESS. Fighting Order with greatcoat rolled.

13. Each Gun Detachment will if possible consist of 1 N.C.O. and six men. Section Officers to inform Orderly Room by 9.0. a.m. on the 7th inst the strength of their section in the line.

14. Two days rations will be carried by all ranks to the line, and rations in future will be issued every alternate day.

15. Three petrol tins per section will be taken, refilling - good local supplies same will be brought up with rations.

16. **CARRIERS.** All be done in Coy time. The present Company has had no trouble.
Two Carriers will be obtained if possible for guns 13 & 14.

17. Brigade Headquarters at T.1.a.6.7. and forward report centre at ....

18. Corporal Signaller will be responsible for sending note to Transport Officer with returning transport stating the amount of ammunition to be handed over to 14th M.G.Coy. at their transport lines.

19. The Second in Command will also inform the Transport Officer the number of filled belt boxes to be handed over to 14th M.G.Coy. on completion of relief.

20. **RUNNERS.** One runner for K.O.S.B. Battalion to be at Company Headquarters on completion of relief, and one runner each from 13 & 14 and 15 & 16.

21. Lists of trench stores taken over will be forwarded to Company Headquarters with relief complete report.

22. Headquarters will consist of C.O. second in command, Sergeant Major, two Orderly Room Staff, L. Cpl and 4 Signallers, 1 Batman, 1 Officers Mess Cook, 1 Company Cook and 6 runners. Cook will take two dixies to Company Headquarters.

23. Nos. 1 & 4 A.M. positions are Army positions. Nos. 2 & 3 are Company positions.

24. Intelligence Report, Casualty Return, Ration Strength, Report of Work Done and proposed ammunition expended and material required will be sent to Company Headquarters by 9.0. a.m. daily.

25. All spare section gear will be left on the dump at .... in charge of the Q.M.S.

Copy No. 1. to O.C. Company.
  "   " 2. "   "   "   No. 1 Section.
  "   " 3. "   "   "   "   2. "
  "   " 4. "   "   "   "   3. "
  "   " 5. "   "   "   "   4. "
  "   " 6. "   "   "   Transport Section.
  "   " 7. "   "   War Diary.
  "   " 8. "   Adjt. M.G.Coy.

                                        Lieut for Major.
                                  Commanding 13th Machine Gun Company.

23/4/5.

Copies to be destroyed by C.O. on 8/10/17.
a Report to this effect sent to C.H.Q.
by C.O. and Runner. (Sgd) E.R.M.K. Major.

APPENDIX V

SECRET.   REMNANT COMPANY ORDER No. 32.   Appx V   Copy No. 7.

Ref Maps No.5. 3rd Edtn.   Oct.13th. 1917.
        NIEUPORT.

                    The following moves will take place this evening.

1.   W. Section will be evacuated complete with guns and all equipment, less belt boxes (the equivalent of which they will receive at the ration dump, half from X and half from Z Section) and will move to Transport Lines with returning ration limber at 5.0.p.m. tonight.
       Sgt. Ellor is responsible that his Section does not move in a formed body till dusk, if any enemy planes or balloons are up, in any case they are not to be in a closer formation than file in half Sections.

2.   No. 11 & 12 positions with the exception of guns and tripods will be taken over by the present Nos. 15 & 16 guns under Sgt Brunswick who will be under the tactical order of Lieut Kelly and will arrange to draw the rations for Guns Nos. 13 & 14 as heretofore.
       Sgt Brunswick will arrange to move during today or at dusk the bulk ammunition from 15 & 16 positions and place it on a M.G. S.A.A. Dump to be formed by Lieut.Kelly. Sgt. Brunswick will arrange to send his belt boxes by driblets to the vicinity of the ration dump to be taken over by W. Section at 5.p.m to-day.

3.   Nos. 5 & 6 positions will be evacuated by Lieut. Kelly less belt boxes, bulk ammunition and trench stores and these guns will go into positions Nos. 9 & 10 previously evacuated by W. Section.
       Trench stores from Nos 15 & 16 positions will be absorbed in the trench stores of Nos. 9, 10, 11 & 12 positions as Lieut. Kelly may order.

4.   X. Section will evacuate positions 1, 2 & 3 and will move No.3 complete with trench stores, bulk and belt ammunition to new No.3 Post at M.30.d.65.05. O.C. X Section will arrange for the bulk ammunition from Nos. 1. & 2. positions to be moved and placed on the Section Dump formed by Lieut Kelly(see para 2).
       Trench stores of Nos.1 & 2 positions will be absorbed in Positions 3.4.5 & 6 as directed by 2/Lieut Fisher.
       Guns and tripods from 1.2.3. will take over positions Nos.5 & 6 from Y. Section.
       Accommodation for Nos.3 & 4 and 2/Lieut Fisher has been arranged direct.
       2/Lieut Fisher will arrange with Lieut Kelly that the belt boxes from Nos. 1 & 2 positions are moved to the vicinity of of X. Sections Headquarters preparatory to there being evacuated by W. Section this evening.
       X. Section Guns at Nos. 5 & 6 positions will be under the tactical order of Lieut Kelly.

5.   Pending further instructions the present A.A. positions will be maintained by day.

6.   Trench pump on charge of Nos. 15 & 16 Guns will be transferred from thence to No.3 position.

7.   Lieut Kelly is responsible that the evacuation of W. Section is carried out in small parties and not the whole Section at the same time.

8. Lists of trench stores and ammunition on new S.A.A. Dump will be forwarded to Company Headquarters on the morning of the 14th inst.

9. Lieut Reynolds will spend the night of 13/14th inst with O.C. Y Section and on the 14th inst will take over from 2/Lieut Fisher, and assume command of X. Section.

    2/Lieut Fisher after handing over will proceed to Transport Lines and assume command of W Section.

10. New S.O.S. Lines attached. Section Officers concerned are responsible that their guns are laid on the new S.O.S. Line by dusk.

11. Relief Complete to be reported by O.C. X & Y Sections and Sgt Brunswick on completion.

    Sgt Ellor to report arrival at Transport Lines by wire using O.F.

12. Copies Nos. 1.2.3.4 & 5 to be destroyed and a certificate rendered to this effect.

Please Acknowledge.

Copy No. 1. to O.C. X. Section.
"   " 2. " " Y. "
"   " 3. " " Z. "
"   " 4. " N.C.O. 1/c W. Section.
"   " 5. "   "   15 & 16 Guns.
"   " 6. " War Diary.
"   " 7. "   "
"   " 8. " Headquarters REACH.

E R M Kirkpatrick

Major.
Commanding REMNANT.

Time... 12.20 p.m. 13/10/17
By... Runner

APPENDIX. VI.

SECRET.   Copy No. 4

REMNANT COMPANY ORDER No. 35.

Ref. Map. No.5. 3rd Edition   15th. Oct. 1917.
NIEUPORT.

1.   Two detachments Y Section under Lieut Kelly will relieve
      two detachments Z Section in Nos. 13 & 14 Positions at dusk
      tonight.

2.   The two detachments Z Section relieved from
      13 & 14 Positions will take up positions 7 & 8 vacated by
      Y Section.

3.   The personnel at positions 9 & 10 will move and take over
      positions 11 & 12 and the personnel at 11 & 12 will take over
      positions 9 & 10. The adjustment will place Z Section in positions
      7,8,9, & 10. with two detachments Y Section in positions 11 & 12.
      No Guns or Equipment will be removed.

4.   O.C. Y Section with the No.1 of his detachments concerned and
      a guide will proceed to the BRICKWORKS during the day to take
      over all particulars concerning the positions. In the same way
      after handing over to O.C. Y Section, O.C. Z Section and his No.1
      concerned will proceed to his new positions, and take over all
      particulars. Guides will be sent back to guide detachments to
      their various positions at dusk.

5.   O.C. Z Section will be in Command of Guns Nos. 7,8,9,10,11 & 12.
      both for tactical and administrative purposes.

6.   All gun equipment including guns, trench stores will be taken
      over in each case.

7.   Completion of relief to be reported to Company Headquarters
      using the letters "O.K.".

8.   Acknowledge.

9.   This Order to be destroyed and Certificate rendered to Company
      Headquarters to this effect.

      Copy No. 1. to O.C. Y. Section.
       "   " 2. " "   Z.   "
       "   " 3. " War Diary.
       "   " 4. "   "   "
       "   " 5. " File.

                                                Lieut for Major,
                                              Commanding REMNANT.

APPENDIX VII

SECRET.   Copy.No...6...

REMNANT COMPANY ORDER No. 37.

Ref Maps No.5. 3rd Edition   16/10/17.
        NIEUPORT.

            The following moves will take place at dusk tonight.

1.   One Section 127th Machine Gun Company will relieve Guns
        No. 5, 6, 7, & 8.

2.   These positions are to be evacuated before dusk, left clean
        and all Trench Stores ~~cleared~~ removed except bulk ammunition
        which Lieut Ramsbottom will hand over to 127 Machine Gun Company
        and obtain receipt.

3.   O.C. Z Section will detail two guides & Sgt Howard to be at
        the T Cross Roads (M.34.a.40.40.) at 6 p.m. tonight to guide
        the incoming Section to their gun-positions.

4.   Guns 5 & 6 complete with all Trench Stores (less bulk S.A.A.
        not required will be handed over to Lieut Ramsbottom for handing
        to 127 Machine Gun Company) will move to positions as arranged
        with Lieut Reynolds in M.30.c.& d.

5.   Guns 7 & 8 complete with all Trench Stores (Less bulk S.A.A.
        not required which will be handed over to Lieut Ramsbottom)
        will move to positions 11 & 12.

6.   Guns No. 11 & 12 under Sgt Gent complete with Trench Stores
        Bulk S.A.A. etc., will relieve four guns of 125 M.G.Coy in the
        Canal Bank about M.29.d.1.6. taking over carefully all S.O.S.
        Lines, Orders etc. These guns will be used for indirect fire.

7.   This adjustment of guns will place Z Section in positions
        9, 10, 11 & 12.

8.   Completion of Relief to be reported to Company Headquarters
        by Runner.

9.   Amended list of Trench Stores to be rendered to Company
        Headquarters after move.

10.   ACKNOWLEDGE.

11.   Destroy this Order when read and understood and send
        Certificate to Company Headquarters to this effect.

        Copy No. 1. to O.C. X Section.
          "   " 2. "   "   Y.   "
          "   " 3. "   "   Z.   "
          "   " 4. " War Diary.
          "   " 5.   War Diary.
          "   " 6.   File.
          "   " 7.   Sgt Gent.
                                                    for Major.
                                              Commanding REMNANT.

SECRET.

APPENDIX VIII

S E C R E T.
NIEUPORT COMPANY ORDER No. 32.

Copy No. 5

Ref Map No. 5. 3rd Edition.   15th Oct. 1917.
NIEUPORT.

1.   W Section under 2/Lieut Fisher will relieve Z Section at dusk ~~to-morrow night~~ *on the night of the 17/18th Oct/17.*

2.   Relief to move up from lines in detachments at 100 yards interval.

3.   Relieving Section will take up positions 9,10,11 & 12 complete with Guns, tripods, petrol tins and all Trench Stores.

4.   2/Lieut Fisher, his Sergeant and one man per gun should arrive about 4.30 p.m. to take over in daylight.
        Relief to commence at 5.15 p.m. and continue as detachments arrive.

5.   Section Headquarters are at H.36.b.9.8.

6.   No guides will meet detachments.

7.   Completion of Relief to be reported to Company Headquarters.

8.   Z Section will proceed to Transport Lines by detachments as relieved.

9.   O.C. W Section will forward List of Trench Stores taken over with the morning reports on the 18th inst.

10.   O.C. W Section to arrange with Transport Officer whether he carries up his two days rations or draws them at the ration dump.

11.   Please Acknowledge.

12.   <u>Destroy</u> this Order when read and understood.

Copy No. 1. to O.C. W. Section.
"   "   2. "   "   Z.   "
"   "   3. " Transport Officer.
"   "   4. " BEACH H.Qrs.
"   "   5. " War Diary.
"   "   6. "   "
"   "   7. " File.

                                                Major.
                                        Commanding NIEUPORT.

APPENDIX. IX

SECRET. Copy No...7...

REMNANT OPERATION ORDER No.42.

Ref Map. No.5. 3rd Edition.
NIEUPORT.   19th October, 1917.

1. The 12th Battery Motor Machine Gun Corps will relieve ~~Nos~~. One Section 126 Machine Gun Company and one Section 127th Machine Gun Company in positions 5.6.7.8.9.10.11 & 12 at dusk tonight the 19th October, 1917.

2. The above positions will be re-numbered and now read Nos. 1 to 8 for Nos. 5 to 12 respectively.

3. Section 127th Machine Gun Company will remove all Gun equipment and make its own arrangements for transport etc.
    After relief this Section will rejoin its Company at a place to be ascertained by Lieut. Barker.

4. O.C. Y Section will hand over all belt boxes to relieving Section and obtain receipts. All other gun equipment to be removed.

5. All Trench Stores, S.O.S. Lines, Calculations and Maps to be handed over and receipts obtained. Copies of same to be forwarded to Company Headquarters with Relief Complete.

6. O.C. relieving Company will hand over to Lieut. Hampson at Transport Lines X.3.c.9.9. (FURNES 1/40,000. provisional issue), the equivalent number of belt boxes handed over.(see para 4.)

7. Guides will be detailed from each detachment to be at PELICAN BRIDGE at 5. p.m. to guide relieving detachments to their gun positions.

8. After relief Y Section will proceed to Transport Lines. Limbers to convey equipment etc., will be at BELGIAN CORNER at 7 p.m. tonight the 19th inst.

9. O.C. 12th Battery Motor Machine Gun Corps will detail one runner to live at Company Headquarters 126 M.G. Coy, to maintain communication with his Section.

10. Completion of relief to be reported to Coy H.Qrs. using the letters "O.K."

11. ACKNOWLEDGE.

12. Destroy this Order when read and understood.

Copy No.1 to H.Qrs. REACH
"   " 2. "   "   RESCUE.
"   " 3. "   "   REAL.
"   " 4. " O.C. Y Section.
"   " 5. " O.C. Section RUT.
"   " 6. " 12th Battery M.M.G.Coy.
"   " 7. " War Diary.
"   " 8.
"   " 9. " O.C Transport

Ernest Fitzpatrick
                                                                Major.
                                                        Commanding REMNANT.

Appendix X

SECRET.   REMNANT ORDER No.46.   Copy No. 9

Reference G.F.1/51 dated 17/10/17.
RANDOM.

1. **S.O.S.**   The S.O.S. and night lines of fire of the
                    Machine Gun Battery in the vicinity of
                    WHITE HOUSE are as follows (See Attached Form 'C'.

2. **ORGANISATION.** The Battery will be divided into 2 Sections of
                    4 guns each - Barrages called :-

                    A.   = 5 guns, and includes 1 gun from position Y.4.
                    B.   = 4 "
                    A.1. = 8 "
                    B.1. = 8 "

3. **LINES OF FIRE.** Guns will be permantly laid, as shewn, on A. and B.
                    but A. may be switched on to B.1., making B.1. a
    total of 8 guns. Similarly, B. may be shifted on to A.1. Barrage
    making a total of 9 guns.
                    If one barrage only is called for and S.O.S. has
    not gone up for the other barrage, O.C.Battery will automatically
    put down the whole 8 guns on the barrage called for.

4. **CO-ORDINATES.** Actual co-ordinates, as near as possible, of guns
                    and centre of cones of fire are shewn on attached
    form and map. Y.4. line of fire cannot be altered - no
    communication.

5. **POSITION OF C.O.** The Officer Commanding this Battery lives at
                    WHITE HOUSE and has a telephone there.

6. **COMMUNICATION.** (a) Communication can be obtained by Left Brigade
                    To O.C. Battery through Right Brigade- Right
    Battalion- WHITE HOUSE, or by runner from REMNANT.
    Left Battalion-Right Brigade communicates through Right Battalion
    to WHITE HOUSE, or by runner. Communication by runner, however,
    should not be relied upon.
                    (b) Communications at present are unsatisfactory
    but it is hoped to better them in the near future.
                    (c) O.C. Battery will send runner to Right
    Battalion Headquarters to take messages and will arrange with O.C.
    Battalion that, (in case his runner for any reason is not there)
    he will deliver messages to him at his Battery position, or at
    WHITE HOUSE as he (the O.C.Battery) may order.

7. **COMPOSITION OF** This Battery is at present manned by the Motor
   BATTERY.   Machine Gun Battery, but in ordinary course of events
                    is found by one Section REMNANT and one Section
    RAIN or RUT according to their position in the line.

8. **CODE CALLS.** It is suggested that the following code be taken
                    into effect in calling for Barrages :-

                    A.   = SOAKEM.
                    A.1. = SOAKEM ONE.
                    B.   = HITEM.
                    B.1. = HITEM ONE.

                    In addition A. or B. barrage will be put down if,
    and when, visual S.O.S. is seen.

9. **PRIORITY.**   It must be clearly understood that A. and B. barrages
                    have Priority, e.g. if A.1. Barrage is put down and a
    call for B. Barrage is received, the extra guns employed in A.1.
    will be taken off and be put down on the B. Barrage, and vice versa.

9. LOOK-OUTS. O.C. Battery will be instructed that if he is putting down either of the "ONE" Barrages he must have two men on the look-out for a visual S.O.S. on A. or B. as the case may be.

10. AMMUNITION. O.C. Battery is responsible for maintaining a sufficient supply of Belt and Bulk Ammunition, the establishment of an Ammunition Dump and Belt-filling Depot, and knowing where he may obtain extra ammunition if required.

11. RATE OF FIRE. The rate of fire will be 200 rounds per minute for 10 minutes and then 50 rounds per minute until the S.O.S. is cancelled or our Artillery dies down.
All guns to traverse 1. degree right and left and depression stops to be arranged for both lines of all guns.

12. BARRAGES READY. It is hoped that this S.O.S. will be taken into effect on the evening of the 21st October, but owing to alterations in gun positions it is not sure that all guns will be able to be taken into use before the morning of the 22nd inst. The safety and accomodation of detachments will be dealt with before improvements of communications.

13. Y.4. O.C. Section finding guns at F.3., F.4., Y.3., and Y.4. will be responsible for the S.O.S. line of Y.4. and extracts of these orders will be issued to him forthwith.

14. ACKNOWLEDGE.

Major.,
21/10/17.   Commanding REMNANT.

COPY No.1 to   RANDOM
     2. "   REACH.
     3. "   Left Bde RANDOM.(To be handed over on relief).
     4. "   Right Battn.REACH (do.   do.   do.   ).
     5. "   Left Battn REACH (do.   do.   do.   ). Map to follow.
     6. "   Right Section RANDOM
     7. "   Left Section RANDOM
     8. "   O.C. Battery. No map.
     9. "   War Diary.   No map.
    10. "   "   No map.
    11. "   File.   No map.

SECRET.   Copy No. 6

REMNANT OPERATION ORDER No. 52.

1. Lieut. Ramsbottom will relieve Lieut. Reynolds in the right sector by 10 a.m. 25/10/17. On relief, Lieut. Reynolds will proceed to Company Headquarters.

2. Receipts to be obtained for all Trench Stores, Orders, Maps etc., and forwarded to Company Headquarters.

3. Z Section will relieve X Section in the line on the night of the 25/26th inst. One N.C.O. or man per detachment will report at Company Headquarters by 3 p.m. on the 25th and will be sent up to Lieut. Ramsbottom.

4. Remainder of Z Section will move in accordance with Lieut. Ramsbottom's order, on relief X Section will proceed independantly to the Transport Lines.

5. All guns and equipment to be taken over.

6. O.C. Z Section will decide whether he will carry his two days rations on the man or whether he will draw it as usual at the ration dump.

7. ACKNOWLEDGE.

8. Relief to be reported by wire and runner.

Copy No. 1. to O.C. X Section.
"   " 2. to N.C.O. i/c "Z Section.
"   " 3. " Lieut. Ramsbottom.
"   " 4. " Transport Officer.
"   " 5. " War Diary.
"   " 6. "   "   "
"   " 7. " File.

23/10/17.

Major.
Commanding REMNANT.

APPENDIX XII.

REMNANT ORDER No. 59.   Copy No. 5.

1. Y Section will relieve W Section in the Left
    Sector on the night of the 27/28th inst.

2. One N.C.O. or man per gun of Y Section will
    arrive at Company Headquarters by 2.0 p.m. 27th.
    and will be sent up to O.C. Y Section.

3. Remainder will arrive with rations. Marching in
    File with 200 yds. between detachments.

4. O.C. W Section will have one guide per detach-
    ment at ration dump to meet Y Section and they
    will be guided to W Section H.Qrs.

5. Detachments of W Section on relief will return
    to Transport Lines.

6. Relief Complete will be reported to C.H.Qrs.,
    by wire and runner.

7. All Trench Stores, S.A.A. etc., will be checked
    and reported as correct. *Guns & Equipment will
    be handed over*

8. 2/Lieut. Barclay will assume Command of Y
    Section on relief complete.

Copy No. 1 to O.C. W. Section.
  "   " 2. " N.C.O. i/c Y. Sect.
  "   " 3. " Transport Officer.
  "   " 4. " War Diary.
  "   " 5. "
  "   " 6. " File.

                                            Major.
27/10/17.   Commanding REMNANT.

APPENDIX.
XIII

REMNANT ORDER NO. 51.   COPY NO. 4

1. X Section with four guns will relieve six guns of the 12 Motor Machine Gun Battery near WHITE HOUSE today.

2. This makes the Battery six guns instead of eight viz 4 guns X Section and 2 guns M.M.G. Battery.

3. Lieut. Reynolds will take charge of X Section when on this duty.

4. One N.C.O. or man per Team will report at Forward Company Headquarters by 2 p.m. today and then proceed to WHITE HOUSE to take over S.A.A. Trench Stores and all S.O.S. Lines and Orders regarding the positions.

5. Arrangements will be made to hand over belt boxes. The M.M.G. Battery will draw belt boxes to replace ones handed over, at REMNANT Rear, who will be advised of the number to hand over.

6. All equipment except belt boxes will be brought by X Section.

7. S.A.A. and Trench Stores of the two positions being vacated by the M.M.G. Battery and not re-occupied will be absorbed in the Trench Stores of the four positions.

8. The limber with the equipment of X Section will proceed to within 100 yards of the BARRICADE at M.35.b.65.30. and not stop as usual at BELGIUM BORDER BRIDGE. A brakesman will be detailed from X Section for this limber who will also act as a guide.

9. The Section will move to the positions near WHITE HOUSE at dusk 200 yards distance between detachments.

10. Receipts for Trench Stores taken over will be sent to Company Headquarters.

11. Relief Complete will be wired, using the letters "O.K".

12. ACKNOWLEDGE.
COPY No. 1 to O.C. TRANSPORT.
         2.   X SECTION.
         3.   12th Bty. M.M.G.
         4 & 5. War Diary.
         6.   FILE.

31/10/17.
                                                    Lieut.
                                        Commanding REMNANT.

Army Form C. 2118.

WAR DIARY
INTELLIGENCE SUMMARY
(Erase heading not required.)

Vol 10

Place	Date	Hour	Summary of Events and Information	Remarks and references to Appendices
			No 126 Machine Gun Company.	
			Vol XX	Ref. Maps.
			Period 1st Nov. 1917.	NIEUPORT. Nos- 3rd Edition
			to 30th Nov 1917.	FRANCE. SHEET 26A. Edition 6 / 40,000
				BETHUNE (enlarged sheet) Edition 6 / 40,000

Instructions regarding War Diaries and Intelligence Summaries are contained in F. S. Regs., Part II. and the Staff Manual respectively. Title Pages will be prepared in manuscript.

Army Form C. 2118. (1)

WAR DIARY
INTELLIGENCE SUMMARY
(Erase heading not required.)

Instructions regarding War Diaries and Intelligence Summaries are contained in F.S. Regs., Part II. and the Staff Manual respectively. Title Pages will be prepared in manuscript.

Place	Date	Hour	Summary of Events and Information	Remarks and references to Appendices
NEWPORT	1/1/17		Two guns in position at N31a 00.10. 16 fire on Dam at T2d 75.95. Our A.A. M.G's fired 2000 rounds.	W/S
	2/1/17		W. Section relieved Z Section in the Right Section at dusk. Remount Order No 64	Appendix I W/S
	3/1/17			W/S
	4/1/17		Our A.A. M.G's fired 750 rounds.	W/S
	5/1/17		Our A.A. M.G's fired 1000 rounds.	W/S
	6/1/17		Our A.A. M.G's fired 1000 rounds.	W/S
	7/1/17 3pm		Our A.A. M.G's fired 2000 rounds. Z Section relieved X Section at Battery Position. X Section relieved Y Section in the Left Section. Remount Order No 65.	W/S Appendix II
	8/1/17		Our A.A. guns fired 500 rounds at enemy aircraft	W/S

Army Form C. 2118.

WAR DIARY
or
INTELLIGENCE SUMMARY
(Erase heading not required.)

Place	Date	Hour	Summary of Events and Information	Remarks and references to Appendices
NIEUPORT	9/10/17		A very quiet day on the front - one AA gun fired 100 rounds SAA at enemy planes.	
	10/10/17		Enemy artillery active throughout - good two AA guns fired 1000 rounds at enemy planes.	
	11/10/17		Enemy artillery quiet throughout - weather poor making gun practice f...	
	12/10/17		Y Section under Lieutenant? been in support of this and of Y Section relieved X Section at the EAST VICTOR at dusk. X Section proceeded to the Transport Lines.	
	13/10/17		Enemy artillery active, observation fair, some gun shells fired into NIEUPORT known places.	
	14/10/17		Enemy artillery quiet, observation poor, during Y Zone action.	
	15/10/17		Enemy shelling around ... throughout - Enemy planes active - Enemy aircraft guns covered Practice SOS at and BATTERY movements fast improvements made in SOS arrangements — markedly good.	
	16/10/17		Enemy artillery very active NIEUPORT shelled heavily. Enemy plane active between off air great numbers during the day.	
	17/10/17		Enemy artillery very quiet especially from NIEUPORT town onwards.	
	18/10/17		On the night of 17/18/19 the 76 MG Coy were relieved by 103 at Transa the relief was completed by 1 am and passed off without incident - Casualties were nil.	Appendix III
	19/10/17		The Company moved to WORMHOUDT AREA arriving at 5.30 am — it entrained Bergues at DUNKIRKE and proceeded by canal up to BERGUES from thence beyond the station to Company moved to the HARD REST.	Appendix IV
	20/10/17			

Army Form C. 2118.

WAR DIARY
or
INTELLIGENCE SUMMARY
(Erase heading not required.)

Instructions regarding War Diaries and Intelligence Summaries are contained in F. S. Regs., Part II. and the Staff Manual respectively. Title Pages will be prepared in manuscript.

Place	Date	Hour	Summary of Events and Information	Remarks and references to Appendices
HARDIFORT	21/10/17		The Company moved by march route to STAPLE and billets for the night.	
STAPLE	22/10/17		Company moved by march route to WARNE. Arrived into billets. Left STAPLE 9 am and arrived destination about 1 pm. Capt STAPLE.	
WARNE	23/10/17		MAJOR. R.A. HELPS arrived and took over command of Company. Conference of C. O's at Brigade HdQrs.	
WARNE	25/10/17 26/10/17		Training and inspection of transport by G.O.C. 126 Inf Bde on 26/10/17.	
WARNE	27/10/17		Company moved by march route to MOLINGHEM. Went into billets for the night.	
MOLINGHEM	28/10/17		Company moved by march route to BETHUNE	

2449 Wt. W14957/M90 750,000 1/16 J.B.C. & A. Forms/C.2118/12.

Army Form C. 2118.

WAR DIARY
INTELLIGENCE SUMMARY
(Erase heading not required.)

Instructions regarding War Diaries and Intelligence Summaries are contained in F. S. Regs., Part II. and the Staff Manual respectively. Title Pages will be prepared in manuscript.

(1)

Place	Date	Hour	Summary of Events and Information	Remarks and references to Appendices
BETHUNE.	29/9/17		Cleaning + checking of gun gear. BETHUNE. heavily shelled during the day	Nil.
"	30/9/17		Training.	Nil.

Watkins Major
Commanding 126 Coy. M.G.C.

RESTANT ORDER No.64.

Copy.No. 4

1. W Section will relieve Z Section in the Right Sector at dusk on the night of 2nd/3rd Nov. 1917.

2. Limber with one brakesman will proceed to PARADISE INN (NEW RATION DUMP).

3. Lieut Ramsbottom will remain in charge of Right Sector.

4. 2/Lieut Fisher will relieve Lieut Ramsbottom on the morning of the 4th inst taking over all orders, receipts for trench stores etc.

5. Lieut. Ramsbottom will report at Company Headquarters by 1 p.m. on the 4th to proceed on leave to ENGLAND.

6. Sgt. Carter will be responsible that -
(1) Four Nos. 1 are sent by 2 p.m. to Company Headquarters to take over Gun Positions.
(2) That W Section is brought up complete with rations and that 200 yards intervals are kept between detachments and that detachments do not move in the observed area before dusk.

7. Lieut Ramsbottom will have four guides at PARADISE INN by 5 p.m. to meet W. Section.

8. Relief Complete advised by code word "O.K".

9. W Section must have their biscuits in the Iron Ration completely renewed before leaving Transport Lines tonight for the line.

10. ACKNOWLEDGE.

Copy No.1 to O.C. Rear H.Qrs.
    2. " " W. Section.
    3. " " Z. Section.
    4. " " War Diary.
    5. " "
    6. File.

2/11/17.

Lieut.
Commanding RESTANT.

Copy No ...6..

REMNANT ORDER No. 65.

1. Z Section will relieve X Section at the Battery Positions this afternoon the 7th November.

2. X Section on being relieved by Z Section will relieve Y Section in the LEFT Sector.

3. Officers will not be relieved.

4. Z Section will bring its own rations on the men and X and Y Sections will carry the balance of their rations on the men.

5. No guns or kit will be changed.

6. Z Section will march up by detachments at 200 yards distances. A guide will meet them at M.35.A.25.70 (Bridge) at 3.0 pm.

7. Y Section on being relieved will proceed by detachments at 200 yards distances to the Transport Lines.

8. Receipts for all gun kit and trench stores will pass between the Section Sergeants.

9. Y Section will send two guides to PARADISE INN at 4.0 pm to guide X Section.

10. X Section will send four Nos.1. to report to LIEUT BARCLAY at 11 am.

11. Relief complete by O.K.

12. ACKNOWLEDGE.

7/11/17.

Lieut.,
Commanding REMNANT.

Copy No 1. to O.C. X. REMNANT.
     2. "   " Y. REMNANT.
     3. "   " Z. REMNANT.
     4. "   " Rear H.Qrs.
   5.& 6." War Diary.
     U. " File.

Приложение VI

S E C R E T. Copy No. 5

126 MACHINE GUN COMPANY ORDER No. 68.

Reference Map - NIEUPORT No.5. 2nd Edition.   17th Nov. 1917.

1. The 126 Machine Gun Company will be relieved by the Machine Guns of the 102nd CHAUSSERS on the night of 18th/19th November 1917.

2. Guides from each detachment will be at Company Headquarters at 5.0 p.m. on the 18th to guide relieving detachments to their gun positins.

3. One man from each sectin of the relieving Unit will report to O.C. W & Z Sections during the day for the purpose of ascertaining all particulars regarding lines of fire: Trenches etc.   (N.B. one section equals two guns).

4. All Defence Schemes, details of Battery Barrages, trench and local area maps, Air Photos and details of work in hand or proposed will be handed over on relief.

5. All Trench Stores except anti-gas equipment, R.E. material, latrine seats and buckets will be removed from the trenches. Receipts to be obtained for all stores handed over and forwarded to Company Headquarters.

6. All bulk S.A.A. and grenades are to be removed from the trenches and placed on the dump near the Battery Position.

7. After relief Sections will proceed independently to the Transport.   Limbers for W & Z Sections to be at BELGIUM CORNER at 8.0 p.m. and for the Battery Position at 7.30 p.m.
Guides will be sent from Sections to meet their limbers and guides to M.35.a.30.50.(on road just E. of ELIZABETH AND ALBERT BRIDGE).   Headquarters Limber to be at Company H.Qrs by 6.30 pm.
O.C. Transport to use his own discretion as to the number of limbers required to move equipment and blankets of various sections.

8. Route for returning Sections and Transport will be via WULPEN BRIDGE.

9. The British S.O.S. Rifle Grenade will remain in force until 12. noon 19th Nov. 1917.

10. All dug-outs, M.G. emplacements and latrines to be left in a clean and sanitary condition

11. Completion of Relief to be reported by runner to present Company Headquarters.

12.   A C K N O W L E D G E.

Copy No.1 O.C. W Section.
 "   " 2 " Z   "
 "   " 3 " BATTERY.
 "   " 4 " REAR H.Qrs.
 "   " 5 & 6. WAR DIARY.
 "   " 7.   FILE.
                              (Sgd). J.F. BLEAKLEY.
                                      CAPTAIN.
               O.C. 126 MACHINE GUN COMPANY.

Copy No. 5

126th Machine Gun Company Order No. 70.

The Company will move to the WORMHOULDT area on the 19th. inst.

      Reveille ...... 4.0 am.
      Breakfast ..... 4.45 "

The Company will parade at 5.30 am ready to move off at 5.45 am and will join the column at X.4.c.1.1. at 6.0 am in OOST DUNKERQUE, the Company marching in rear of the column.

DRESS. The provisional dress will be "Fighting Order" and Steel helmets.
The haversack will be worn on the back, and ground sheet rolled and strapped to the waistbelt below the haversack.
Greatcoats in packs will be carried in the limbers.

BLANKETS. Blankets will be rolled by Sub-sections and loaded on Transport immediately after reveille.

LIMBERS. Limbers will be packed and all stores will be loaded as far as possible on the night of the 18th. inst.

RATIONS. One Days ration will be carried in the haversack.

WATER. All waterbottles are to be filled on the night of the 18th, also dixies will be filled for breakfast requirements. The watercart will then be refilled and noone will be allowed further supply.

STEEL HELMET COVERS. will be removed from helmets and handed in to C.Q.M.S. Stores.

                                  Lieut.,
                                for Captain,
18/11/17.   Commanding 126th Machine Gun Comany.

Copies to :-
      NO.1. - O.C. Company.
      " 2. - Transport Officer.
      " 3. - File.
      " 4. - "
      " 5. - War Diary.
      " 6. - " "

Army Form C. 2118.

WAR DIARY
INTELLIGENCE SUMMARY
(Erase heading not required.)

No. 126. Machine Gun Company

Vol. XXI.

Period 1st Dec 1917
to 31st Dec 1917.

BETHUNE (combined sheet) 40.0.0
LA BASSEE 36cNW1
EDITION 10 A.

Army Form C. 2118.

WAR DIARY
or
INTELLIGENCE SUMMARY
(Erase heading not required.)

Instructions regarding War Diaries and Intelligence Summaries are contained in F. S. Regs., Part II. and the Staff Manual respectively. Title Pages will be prepared in manuscript.

Place	Date	Hour	Summary of Events and Information	Remarks and references to Appendices
BÉTHUNE	1/12/17 to 6/12/17		Company in Corps Reserve and billeted in BÉTHUNE Training	
do	7/12/17 to 10/12/17		Company in Corps Reserve and billeted in BÉTHUNE TRAINING.	Nalt
La Bassée	11/12/17		The Coy relieved the 125 M.G. Coy in the Right sector, Canal Sector.	Appendix I Nalt
	12/12/17		Artillery inactive. Our M.G's fired 2000 rounds S.A.A. on Enemy Posts. Observation fair	Nalt
	13/12/17	10.15pm to 12pm	Enemy fired several hundred gas shells S of CAMBRIN. Our M.G's fired on trenches at A.10.C.65.65. A.16.A.95.93. 3000 rounds were expended.	Nalt
	14/12/17		Observation poor. Enemy Artillery quiet. Our M.G's fired 4500 rounds on A.23.C.10.40. A.10.C.65.65. A.16.A.85.92. A.10.D.95.60.	Nalt
	15/12/17		Observation poor. Artillery inactive. Our M.G's fired 5700 rounds on A.23.A.00.55 - 65.65. A.10.D.35.45 - 85.70.	Nalt
	16/12/17		Enemy artillery below normal. Our artillery inactive. Observation fair. Our M.G's fired 3300 rounds on A.10.B.no.77. A.29.A.90.85.	Nalt
	17/12/17		Enemy artillery shelled VILLAGE LINE heavily 10 am - 12 noon using 5"shells also TOWER RESERVE and MARLEBONE RD 3-4pm (8") Our M.G's fired on A.16.B.20.05 - D.70.50. A.11.C.12.13 - 30.70.	Nalt

WAR DIARY
or
INTELLIGENCE SUMMARY
(Erase heading not required.)

Army Form C. 2118.

Instructions regarding War Diaries and Intelligence Summaries are contained in F. S. Regs., Part II. and the Staff Manual respectively. Title Pages will be prepared in manuscript.

Place	Date	Hour	Summary of Events and Information	Remarks and references to Appendices
La Bassée	18/7/17		Very quiet day. 9.40 am Enemy shelled La Bassée Rd. Artillery below normal. Our Machine Guns fired on enemy targets at A23 C10 to A22 B20 8A. 3800 rounds expended.	N[ote]
	19/7/17		Our Artillery shelled enemy front & support lines at intervals — enemy artillery shelled Tower Reserve & Kingsway, shortly 8-9 pm. Our Machine Guns fired on enemy targets at A23A C9JT, L65 L5, and A10 D35 45. 3800 rounds were expended.	N[ote]
	20/7/17		Artillery normal, shrapnel good, enemy shelled our lines with S.G. shrapnel 8.15-9.15 pm Railway Embankment shelled with 8" shells. Our Machine Guns fired on enemy targets at A11 C10.D.-20.30. A29.A 90 95. 3000 rounds expended.	N[ote]
	21/7/17		Artillery below normal. Our Machine Guns fired on enemy target A17 C10.60. 3000 rounds were expended.	N[ote]
	22/7/17		Enemy artillery active, shelled Railway Embankment 9-10 am Railway Bridge and Cuinchy at 7 Few Our Machine Guns fired on enemy target at A6 B20 65. 3000 rounds were expended. A burst fired any eighth-sight on front of 45 Brigade-HQ	N[ote]
	23/7/17		Our Artillery very active between 2 am & 3 am & 10 am - 12 noon. Enemy artillery below normal. Our Machine Guns fired on enemy targets A22 B20 60. 3000 rounds were expended.	N[ote]
	24/7/17		Our Artillery below normal. Enemy artillery active our rear SG shells. Our M.G.s fired on target A10 D35 45. 3000 rounds were expended.	N[ote]
	25/7/17		Our artillery at 6.30 pm fired on SOS line in answer to SOS call from La Bassée 7.30 pm bombarded enemy line & put mine shaft gas on a 1500x front also at 9.10 pm & 10.30 Our retaliation cost the artillery on certain targets	N[ote]

Army Form C. 2118.

WAR DIARY
or
INTELLIGENCE SUMMARY
(Erase heading not required.)

Instructions regarding War Diaries and Intelligence Summaries are contained in F. S. Regs., Part II. and the Staff Manual respectively. Title Pages will be prepared in manuscript.

Place	Date	Hour	Summary of Events and Information	Remarks and references to Appendices
LA BASSÉE	26/11/17		Artillery on both sides below normal. Our MG's fired on enemy targets at A.29.C.50.70 & A.17.C.10.60. 3000 rounds expended	M.H.
	27/11/17		Our Artillery below normal. Enemy at 11am shelled CAMBRIN with long range guns. Our MG's fired on enemy targets at A.29.C.50.70 & A.17.C.10.60. 3000 rounds were expended	M.H.
	28/11/17		Artillery very quiet. One enemy machine gun was located firing from RYAN'S KEEP. Our MG's fired on targets at A.28.B.60.60 A.16.B.20.05—d.70.50. 3000 rounds expended.	M.H.
	29/11/17		Artillery about normal. Enemy fires 50 5.9 shells on WOLFE RD and buildings at A.8.D.7.3. Our MG's fired on targets at A.22.B.20.75 & A.23.C.10.00. 3000 rounds were expended	M.H.
	30/11/17	8AM—9PM 2.30PM 8.30PM	Our bombs were fired on our front & support lines in front of CUINCHY. GIVENCHY shelled with 5.9 shells. BRICKSTACK & COLDSTREAM LANE gun bombed at A.23.A.10.35 & A.10.D.35.45. Our MG's fired on enemy targets at A.23.A.10.35 & A.10.D.35.45	M.H.
	3/12/17		Artillery normal. Our MG's fired on enemy targets at A.29.A.90.85 & A.11.C.12.12—20.30. 3000 rounds expended.	M.H.

[signature] MAJOR
Comdg 126 MG Coy.

Appendix
I

126 MACHINE GUN COMPANY ORDER No. 75.

Copy No. ...4......

1. The Company will relieve the 125 M.G.Coy in the Right Sector on the 11th inst.

2. A motor lorry will be at the C.Q.M.S. Stores at 7.0 a.m. on the morning of the 10th inst and all stores not in urgent use will be dumped at the C.Q.M.S. Stores at 6.45 a.m. on the morning of the 10th as per detailed instructions to Company Sergeant Major. One blanket per man will be rolled tightly in bundles by detachments and dumped at the C.Q.M.S.Stores by 6.45 a.m. on the morning of the 10th. C.S.M. will detail 1 N.C.O. and 3 men to accompany the wagon as guard, rationed including the 11th.

3. The Company will move in two parties on the 11th inst.
1st Party to consist of :-

A Group. (No.1 limber of Z Section with 4 guns of Z Section and 2 guns of Y Section complete with 6 tripods, 2 spare part boxes, 6 oil wallets, 6 spare part wallets and condensers etc.

B Group. (No.1 limber of W Section with 4 guns of W Section and 1 gun of Y Section equipped similar to No.1 limber of Z Section.

C Group. (No. 1 limber of X Section with 4 guns of X Section and 1 gun of Y Section equipped similar to Z Section.

Teams to consist of 5 men per gun - four of whom will remain with their guns and one will return to Company H.Qrs after ascertaining position of his guns.

4. The Nos 1 of each team will proceed to 125 M.G.Coy H.Qrs. PREOL at 2.0 p.m. on the afternoon of the 10th inst to view the line, they will carry balance of day's ration and next day's ration. Lieut. Ramsbottom will be in charge of A Group.
2/Lieuts Fisher and Hough " " " " " B "
2/Lieuts Barclay and Barnet " " " " " C "

5. This party will parade at 7.45 a.m. to move off at 8.0 a.m. on the morning of the 11th inst. Guides will meet the party at 125 M.G.Coy H.Qrs PREOL.

6. The Second Party *WILL PARADE* at 1.15 p.m. on the 11th inst to move off at 1.30 p.m. and will consist of the nucleus of the Company and Transport and will proceed to 125 M.G.Coy H.Qrs at PREOL. Blankets to be rolled in bundles by detachments, labelled and put on G.S. wagon by 7.0 a.m. on the 11th inst.

7. Rations will continue to be drawn at the same place as usual by 1st Line Transport.

8. Belt boxes and bulk ammunition will be handed over by 125 M.G.Coy.

9. DRESS. Fighting Order with haversacks on back, greatcoats rolled and fastened by valise straps under the haversack, waterproof sheets under flap of haversack, jerkins to be worn over tunics.

10. Receipts for trench stores to be sent to Company Headquarters. Billets to be left scrupulously clean.
Relief Complete to be advised by runner with Code Word "O.K".

11. Orders re rations to be carried on the man will be issued on the 10th.

Major.

9/12/17.   Commanding 1 26 Machine Gun Company.

Army Form C. 2118.

Confidential

Vol 12

WAR DIARY
INTELLIGENCE SUMMARY.
(Erase heading not required.)

No. 126 M. Gun. Coy.

VOL XXIII

PERIOD 1st JAN 1918
TO
13th JAN 1918

REF MAPS
BÉTHUNE (COMBINED SHEET) 40 000 / 1
LA BASSÉE 36c NW¼ 1/10000
EDITION 10 A.
RICHEBOURG 36 S.W.3 1/10000
Section 9A

Army Form C. 2118.

WAR DIARY
INTELLIGENCE SUMMARY.
(Erase heading not required.)

Instructions regarding War Diaries and Intelligence Summaries are contained in F. S. Regs., Part II. and the Staff Manual respectively. Title pages will be prepared in manuscript.

Place	Date	Hour	Summary of Events and Information	Remarks and references to Appendices
LA BASSEE	1/1/18		Our artillery fired salvoes during the day. Enemy artillery normal. Our MG's fired on enemy targets at A.29.C.50.70 & A.17.C.10.60. 3000 rounds were expended	N/A
	2/1/18	8.30 to 10.30 p.m.	our artillery bombarded enemy trenches Kiosles. Enemy normal – Our MG's fired on enemy targets at A.16.B.20.05 – at 70.50 & A.28.B.60.80. 3000 rounds were expended	N/A
	3/1/18	9.40	Our naval guns fired 10 rounds into AUCHY. – Enemy gas shelled KINGSCLERE at 9 am	N/A
		11 am	KINGSWAY shelled with 8" at 9.20 pm Our MG's fired on enemy targets at A.29.A.25.00 & A.17.C.25.75. 3000 rounds were expended	
	4/1/18		Coy was relieved by 127 MG Coy in the CANAL SECTOR and proceeded to billets at ESSARS	APPENDIX I N/A
ESSARS	5/1/18		Inspection of Kit and equipment.	N/A
"	6/1/18		Church parade	N/A
"	7/1/18		Inspection of sections by O.C. Company & Fancey.	N/A
"	8/1/18		Holiday – Christmas celebrations	N/A
"	9/1/18		Working party of 1 officer & 70 O.R. at 42nd Bri. R.E. dump BEUVRY. Relief of the Sector at the BREWERY CORNER. FESTUBERT.	N/A

WAR DIARY
or
INTELLIGENCE SUMMARY.
(Erase heading not required.)

Army Form C. 2118.

Place	Date	Hour	Summary of Events and Information	Remarks and references to Appendices
ESTAIRS	10/1/18		Working party of 1 off & 70 O.R. at 42nd Div. R.E. dump BEUVRY. Inspection of transport by G.O.C. 126 Inf Bde & Lt Col Coulson 42nd Div. Train.	WW
"	11/1/18		Company Training.	WW
"	12/1/18		Working party of 1 Officer & 70 O.R. at 42nd Div. R.E. dump BEUVRY. 126th Brigade Transport Competitions in afternoon.	WW
"	13/1/18		Church Parade. Working party pt consisting of 1 Officer & 60 O.R. for work on VILLAGE LINE GIVENCHY SECTOR. Relief of section at BREWERY CORNER FESTUBERT.	WW
"	14/1/18 15/1/18		Company training	WW
"	16/1/18		Working party of 1 Officer & 70 O.R. for work on VILLAGE LINE GIVENCHY SECTOR	WW
"	17/1/18		Training. Preparation for relief on the 18th.	WW

Army Form C. 2118.

WAR DIARY
INTELLIGENCE SUMMARY.
(Erase heading not required.)

Instructions regarding War Diaries and Intelligence Summaries are contained in F. S. Regs., Part II and the Staff Manual respectively. Title pages will be prepared in manuscript.

Place	Date	Hour	Summary of Events and Information	Remarks and references to Appendices
ESSARS.	18/1/18		The Company relieved the 125th Machine Gun Company in the GIVENCHY SECTOR of the line in the early morning. COMPANY HQRS at LE PLANTIN.	Appendix II
LE PLANTIN	19/1/18		Our machine guns fired during the night, harassing fire on :- 1. Gasworks at A4 c 65.05. 2. Trenches A4 c 30.52 to A4 c 20.90 3. Suspected HQRS A4 c 65.30. 4070 rds L.S.A.A. expended	
"	20/1/18		Our machine guns expended 4070 rds S.A.A. during the day and night on REDOUBT ALLEY SOUTH and on CROSS ROADS (A10a 70.80). Quiet throughout the day on the Front. Enemy machine guns active at night.	
"	21/1/18		Quiet throughout the day. Usual machine gun fire at night on tracks and trenches behind the enemy lines - 5500 rds S.A.A. expended	
"	22/1/18		Nothing to report	

A5834 Wt.W4973/M687 750,000 8/16 D. D. & L. Ltd. Forms/C.2118/13.

Army Form C. 2118.

WAR DIARY
INTELLIGENCE SUMMARY
(Erase heading not required.)

Place	Date	Hour	Summary of Events and Information	Remarks and references to Appendices
LE PLANTIN	23/1/18	—	Our guns fired during the night on A10 a 70·80 and harassed from A10 62580 G. A10 to 80 70 and during the day on REDOUBT ALLEY SOUTH. Enemy quiet during the day but a great success in enemy machine gun activity at night has been observed for the last ten nights	Walt
"	24/1/18		Nothing to report. Our guns fired harassing fire at usual during the night & day	Walt
"	25/1/18		Nothing to report during day. Enemy planes very active at night bombing the back areas.	Walt
"	26/1/18		Harassing fire by our machine guns during the day night onto on tracks & road junctions behind the enemy's lines	Walt
"	27/1/18		Quiet throughout the day. Enemy TM's rather more active about GIVENCHY. Our machine guns fired during the day night on the usual targets behind the enemy's lines	Walt

Army Form C. 2118.

WAR DIARY
or
INTELLIGENCE SUMMARY

(Erase heading not required.)

Instructions regarding War Diaries and Intelligence Summaries are contained in F. S. Regs., Part II. and the Staff Manual respectively. Title Pages will be prepared in manuscript.

Place	Date	Hour	Summary of Events and Information	Remarks and references to Appendices
LE PLANTIN	28/1/18		Nothing to report	Nil
"	29/1/18		Inspection of Transport at Rear HQrs. by G.O.C. 126 Inf. Bde. One machine gun fired during the night on enemy works destroying transport by artillery fire. An experiment was carried out with the above gun, firing without the clock cover. The gun fired fairly well at the normal rate of fire with the Tuzzee spray at 4½ to b1 cemented vaporty	Nil
"	30/1/18		One section 268th M.G. Coy occupied position in the VILLAGE LINE in this sector, relieving one of our detachments. After relief this detachment occupied position LEPS. 4. Our machine guns fired during the night on RIdel 9565	Nil
"	31/1/18		Nothing to report	

Watkins Major.
Commanding 126. Coy. Machine Gun Corps

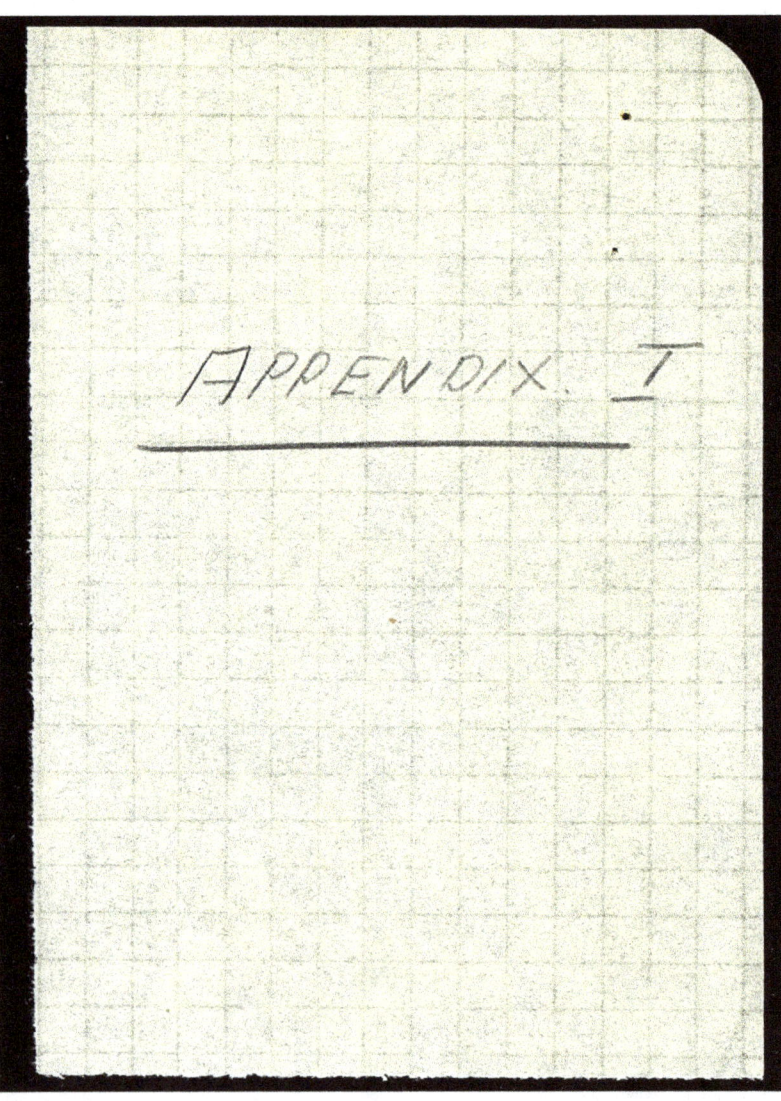

Copy No........ 9.

146 MACHINE GUN COMPANY ORDER No. 78.

1. The 147th. M.G.Coy will relieve 146th. M.G.Coy in the CANAL SECTOR defences at 2 p.m. 3rd. January, 1918.

2. **Z Section.** At 9.0 a.m. 3/1/18 one guide from each sub-section will be at PONT PINS to conduct the relieving detachments to V.48 a 25 and the PONT PINS positions respectively.
   No.147 Company's limber will remain near PONT PINS. On completion of relief Z Section 146 Coy will load their guns on this limber and proceed to BATTERY CORNER at FERMICOURT where they will relieve a section of the 147th Company.
   Lieut. Ramsbottom will arrange for guides from A.14.A. & C.B. to be at PONT PINS at 6.0 a.m. 4/1/18 to conduct relieving detachments to their gun positions, on completion of relief these detachments will move to PONT PINS where they will rejoin W & X Section.

3. **Y Section.** Guides from Y Section will be at No.7 RAILWAY BRIDGE at 9.0 a.m. 4/1/18 and will conduct the detachments of 147th Company to their gun positions. On completion of relief guns will be loaded into limbers at CAMBRIN KEEP and will move to Company H.Qrs. at HOSARD.

4. **W & X SECTIONS.** One guide per section will be at PONT FIXE at 9.0 a.m. 4/1/18 and will guide the relieving detachments of 147th Company to CULBUCKHAM TUNNEL & HANOVER CROWN respectively.
   W Section will arrange two guides in addition to meet the incoming detachments at CULBUCKHAM TUNNEL.
   X Section will arrange one guide to meet the detachments for F.4 at HANOVER CROWN. On completion of relief Sections will move independently to PONT PINS and return with limber to HOSARD after picking up detachments from A.14.A. & C.B.

5. Belt boxes, bulk S.A.A. and trench stores will be handed over in all cases. Receipts for trench stores to be obtained in triplicate one copy to be handed to relieving officer.

6. Relief complete to be wired (code word "O.K." used) to Company Headquarters at HOSARD.

7. All Sections will move by detachments at 100 yards distance until West of a line drawn N & S through Brigade H.Qrs.

8. **TRANSPORT.** Two limbers will be at PONT FIXE at 11.0 a.m. 4/1/18. One limber at CAMBRIN KEEP 11.0 a.m. 4/1/18.

Copy No.1. to Coy Headquarters.
"   " 2. " O.C. W Section.
"   " 3. " "   X   "
"   " 4. " "   Y   "
"   " 5. " "   Z   "
"   " 6. " "   Transport.
"   " 7. " File.
"   " 8 & 9. War Diary.

2/1/18.   Major.
                                    Commanding 146 Machine Gun Company.

Copy No...6.

1st MACHINE GUN COMPANY ORDER No. 70.

1. 1st Machine Gun Company will move to HUBARD on morning of the 4th. inst.

2. A motor lorry will be drawn from BEAVRY STATION (LE QUESNOY) 8.15 a.m. on 3rd inst. A guide to be detailed by C.S.M. to reach BEAVRY Station by 8.0 a.m. on 3rd inst to bring this lorry to LE PREOL.

3. C.Q.M.S. will arrange that his dump together with all surplus Mess Stores, Cooks etc., are ready to be loaded on this lorry at 8.0 a.m. on the 3rd inst.
   The C.S.M. will detail 1 N.C.O. & 3 men to rear party this lorry and to act as guard untill the arrival of the Company at HUBARD.

4. The details of Company at present at LE PREOL will fall in at 9.45 a.m. ready to move off at 10.0 a.m. on the morning of 4th inst.
   DRESS. :-   full marching order with steel helmets.

5. Refilling point and time of refilling remain unchanged.

6. Mobile S.A.A. will be handed over to incoming Unit.
   C.Q.M.S. will be informed of number of boxes to be handed over when the information is available.
   The C.Q.M.S. will be informed as to the disposal of the rations of the Section attached to 1st Company when the information is available.

7. Billets, Cookhouses, Latrines &c., will be left scrupulously clean and certificates to this effect will be obtained from the incoming unit.

Lieut.
for Major,
Commanding 1st Machine Gun Company.

2/5/18.

Copy No. 1 to O.C. Transport.
"   " 2 " C.S.M.
"   " 3 " C.Q.M.S.
"   " 4 " File.
"   " 5 " War Diary.

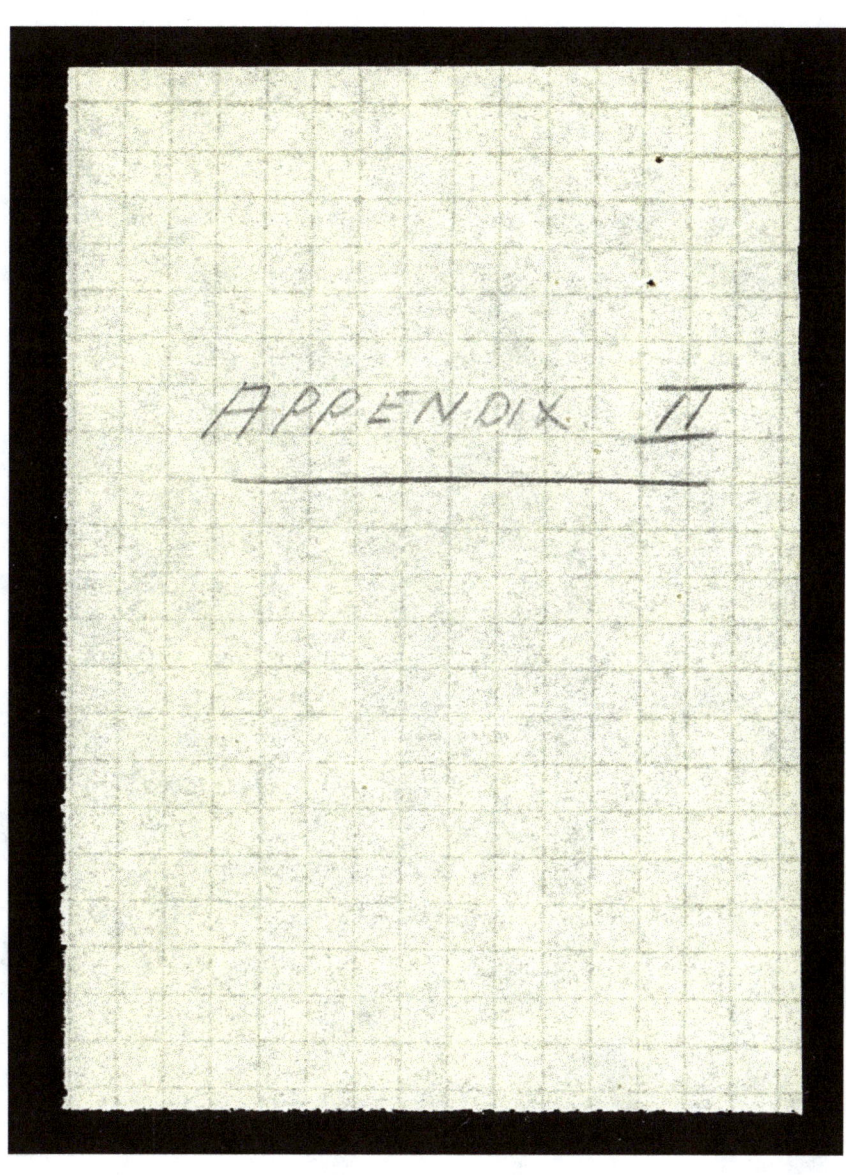

1st LONDON GUN COMPANY ORDER No. 77.

Ref Maps. BETHUNE (combined sheet) 1/40000
LACASSE 36 C.N.W.1. 1/10000   15-1-15.

1. The 12 C R.G.Coy will relieve the 189th M.G.Coy in the GIVENCHY Sector on the morning of the 18th January, 1918.

2. A Section will relieve a section of 189th M.G.Coy at the Centre Battery Position.

3. One Sub-Section of Y Section will relieve a Sub-Section of 189th Company in CANADIAN ORCHARD.

4. Guides will meet the above six gun teams at PRESIDENT CORNER (A.2.d.90.90), at 6.0 a.m.

5. The remaining Sub-Section of Y Section will relieve a Sub-Section of 189th M.G.Coy in position in the VILLAGE LINE.

6. Z Section will relieve a Section of 189th M.G.Coy in GIVENCHY.

7. Guides will meet the above six guns at MARION CORNER (A.1.b.70.90) at 6.0 a.m.

8. Relief Complete to be reported to Company Headquarters in LA PLANTIN.

9. Gun Bases and all trench stores will be handed over, and copies of receipts will be forwarded to Company Headquarters by midday on the 17th inst.

10. W Section at present at the WORMHY FORTRESS will exchange positions with the right battery of 189th M.G.Coy on the 18th inst. Completion of this relief will be forwarded to H.Qrs. 189th Coy at LA PLANTIN.

11. ORDER OF MARCH. X,Y & Z Sections will parade at Company H.Qrs GORRE at 5.30 a.m. on the 18th inst. They will move in two parties consisting of:-
    (a) X Section and Sub Section Y Section going to CANADIAN ORCHARD with one limber under 2/Lieuts. DOUGHTY and HOMER. This limber will return to Rear H.Qrs at GORRE after unloading.
    (b) One Sub-Section of Y Section and Z Section under Lieut. PENNINGTON.
    Both parties will march via GORRE to the JULIAN FORK. First Party (a)will then proceed by the NORTH branch of the JULIAN FORK to PRESIDENT CORNER, the second party (b) taking the SOUTH branch to MARION CORNER. Lieut.Pennington's limber will return to Rear H.Qrs GORRE after unloading.

12. Company H.Qrs will fall in outside Orderly Room at 6.45 a.m. and march following the route of (b) Party above to LA PLANTIN.

13. Transport and remaining details of Company under Lieut. HARRISON and 2/Lieut. BARCLAY will fall in at Company Headquarters at 7.30 a.m. and march to Rear H.Qrs 189th M.G.Coy at GORRE.

14. TRANSPORT. Teams for two Fighting Limbers to be at Wagon Lines at 5.15 a.m. on the 18th inst.
    Team for one Fighting Limber to be at Wagon Lines at 6.15 a.m.

15. Packs of all men going up the line except Headquarters will be stacked at Q.M.S.Stores by noon on the 17th inst.
    All Blankets will be rolled and tied in pens and stacked at Q.M.S.Stores at the same hour.

16.   The unexpended portion of the day's ration will be carried on the men.

17.   Rations will be drawn from the refilling point as hitherto and sent up to advanced Company Headquarters every evening at dusk.

18.   All M.G./Stores will be loaded into limber by 6.0 p.m. on the 10th inst.

19.   RATIONS ANMN.   Rations left M.A.A. and A/A belt boxes will be handed over to D 8th Company. 7,000 rnds bulk M.A.A. will be taken over at GOURY and one belt boxes in the trenches.

20.   BILLETS.   Billets will be left in a clean and sanitary condition and receipts obtained for same. 2/Lieut. BARCLAY and a party of N.C.O. will remain behind and hand over billets, afterwards proceeding to GOURY.

Kastrups
Major.

Commanding 100 Machine Gun Company.

Copy No.1 to O.C. Y Section.
    2.   "   "   X   "
    3.   "   "   Y   "
    4.   "   "   Z   "
    5.   War Diary.
    6.   File.
    7.   O.C. 1/4 M.G.Coy.
    8.   O.C. 1st M.G.Coy.

Army Form C. 2118.

WAR DIARY
of
INTELLIGENCE SUMMARY.
(Erase heading not required.)

No. 126 MACHINE GUN COY.

VOL. XXIII.

PERIOD 1st February 1918
to
28th February 1918

REF. MAPS.

LA BASSEE 36 N.W.1 } 1/10,000
Edition 10A

RICHEBOURG 36 S.W.3 } 1/10,000
Edition 10A

Instructions regarding War Diaries and Intelligence Summaries are contained in F. S. Regs., Part II. and the Staff Manual respectively. Title pages will be prepared in manuscript.

Place	Date	Hour	Summary of Events and Information	Remarks and references to Appendices

Army Form C. 2118.

WAR DIARY
or
INTELLIGENCE SUMMARY.
(Erase heading not required.)

Instructions regarding War Diaries and Intelligence Summaries are contained in F.S. Regs., Part II. and the Staff Manual respectively. Title pages will be prepared in manuscript.

Place	Date	Hour	Summary of Events and Information	Remarks and references to Appendices
LE PLANTIN	1/2/18		Our machine guns fired during the night on A4c 92.10 to A4d 45.70 and during the day on: A10a 52.98 & A10a 95.60 and harassed up and 6. A10a 85.96.	
"	2/2/18		Very quiet on the Front. During the day & night our 4 guns fired salvos aimed fire on 6. Area A4a 49.75 & S.28c 40.15 and on tracks behind the enemy's lines. Visibility improved about 11 am and artillery activity increased	9/15
"	3/2/18		During the night & day our guns fired on various targets behind the enemy's lines, expending 3,500 rounds. Enemy rather more active. Particularly with his machine guns during the night on tracks & strong points behind our lines	9/15
"	4/2/18 5/2/18 6/2/18		Nothing to report. Our guns fired as usual on various targets behind the enemy's lines during the day & night	9/15

Army Form C. 2118.

(2)

WAR DIARY
or
INTELLIGENCE SUMMARY.
(Erase heading not required.)

Instructions regarding War Diaries and Intelligence Summaries are contained in F. S. Regs., Part II. and the Staff Manual respectively. Title pages will be prepared in manuscript.

Place	Date	Hour	Summary of Events and Information	Remarks and references to Appendices
LE QUENTIN	8/2/18		Desultory M.G. fire day and night on machine guns fired on A7c92.10.65 and A7c45.70 and during the day on A7c 58.31, expending 3500 rounds position of gun.	
"	9/2/18		13 O.R. arrived as reinforcement from M.G.C. Base Depot. Our guns fired during the night & day on various targets behind the enemy's lines.	
"	10/2/18		3500 rounds fired by our machine guns on A10 & 65.85 and A7xc 58.31 during the day & night. Several hostile planes engaged during the day by machine guns. Our artillery has been very active during the day cutting the wire in front of the enemy's front line system	
"	11/2/18		Our machine guns supported a raid made by the 9th Manchester Regt on MACKENSEN TRENCH with overhead indirect fire on to various points behind the enemy's lines, as follows:— X 4 guns at A72a 50.70 firing on embankment in A.10.a where enemy machine guns are suspected to keep down any hostile m.g. fire (see X)	

WAR DIARY
or
INTELLIGENCE SUMMARY.

(Erase heading not required.)

Army Form C. 2118.

Place	Date	Hour	Summary of Events and Information	Remarks and references to Appendices
		Contd.	From this direction. 2 guns at I.21.c.65.10 to enfilade Road in A.11a.w.c. to deal with any enemy movement. One gun pushed forward in DEAD MAN'S TRENCH at about A.9.a.80.90 to deal with any enemy machine gun which might attack our raiding party on the flank. ∴ Guns opened fire at Zero (6.15 p.m.) and fired at the rate of 80 rounds per minute expending 12000 rounds.	
LE PLANTIN	13/2/18		3500 rounds were fired during the day on our right on A.10.B.30.75 and on I.28.c.56.61 & I.29.a.10.52. Very Quiet. Nothing to report. Our guns fired as soon as enough ?? the enemy lines	
LE PLANTIN LA BEUVRIERE	14/2/18		We were relieved by the 16.5. M.G. Company. Relief complete by 9.30 p.m. The Company then marched to Billets at LABEUVRIERE	

WAR DIARY
or
INTELLIGENCE SUMMARY.
(Erase heading not required.)

Army Form C. 2118.

Instructions regarding War Diaries and Intelligence Summaries are contained in F.S. Regs., Part II. and the Staff Manual respectively. Title pages will be prepared in manuscript.

Place	Date	Hour	Summary of Events and Information	Remarks and references to Appendices
LA BEUVRIERE	15/2/18		The 42nd Machine Gun Battalion was formed under the command of Lt COLONEL TILLIE M.C. and included this Company in its establishment. The day was devoted to cleaning guns, equipment &c.	N/S
LA BEUVRIERE	16/2/18		Bathing and general cleaning up of guns & equipment	N/S
LA BEUVRIERE	17/2/18		Church Parade.	N/S
LA BEUVRIERE	18/2/18		Checking deficiencies of gun equipment. Second Lieutenant All N.C.O.s paraded under Capt Smith DEVLIN (attd from Division) for bayonet fighting in the afternoon.	N/S
LA BEUVRIERE	19/2/18		Company training during the morning and early afternoon. N.C.O.s paraded in the shops. Officers, N.C.O.s & men lectured by O.C. Battalion	N/S
LA BEUVRIERE	20/2/18		Company training in the morning.	N/S
LA BEUVRIERE	21/2/18		Company training. N.C.Os. paraded on parade. 6 attendants sent & marched men transferred to 127 to E Coy.	N/S
LA BEUVRIERE	22/2/18		Company training. N.C.Os paraded as usual. Lecture by O.C. Battalion to Officers and N.C.Os. Lecture by M.O. on skin disease.	N/S

Army Form C. 2118.

WAR DIARY
or
INTELLIGENCE SUMMARY.
(Erase heading not required.)

Instructions regarding War Diaries and Intelligence Summaries are contained in F. S. Regs., Part II. and the Staff Manual respectively. Title pages will be prepared in manuscript.

Place	Date	Hour	Summary of Events and Information	Remarks and references to Appendices
LA BEUVRIERE	23/3/18		Training – Company training. Musketry – sports. 9 Reinforcements arrived from No. 6. E. Con Depot.	
LA BEUVRIERE	24/3/18		Church Parade	
LA BEUVRIERE	25/3/18		Training – Company training. Musketry – Baths. NCOs parade as usual. Relieved Rams E.R.M. class communication. LIEUT McLACHLAN and 2/LIEUT ESSEX joined company from Base Depot.	
LA BEUVRIERE	26/3/18		Reconnaissance of our ground VIEILLE CHAPELLE by Officers NCos & numbered, with a view to occupy position in event of enemy Company paraded under Coy ? to transport Equip. and Sergeant Gunnery.	
LA BEUVRIERE	27/3/18		Company Training. Relief in box covers.	
LA BEUVRIERE	28/3/18		Company Training. Inspection of Company by Lieut Col TILLIE M.C. Inspection of Gun equipment etc. by DADOS 42nd Division. Leave to all ranks by O.C. Battalion. Amusement provided by officers NCOs & men in own Cookhouses. =	

J P Heatley Capt
acting O.C. 126 C. Machine Gun Co.

www.ingramcontent.com/pod-product-compliance
Lightning Source LLC
Chambersburg PA
CBHW081544160426

43191CB00011B/1834